CHRISTOTHERAPY

HEALING THROUGH ENLIGHTENMENT

Bernard J. Tyrrell

A Crossroad Book

THE SEABURY PRESS • NEW YORK

The Seabury Press
815 Second Avenue
New York, N.Y. 10017

Third printing

Copyright © 1975 by Bernard J. Tyrrell
Printed in the United States of America

LIBRARY OF CONGRESS CATALOGING IN PUBLICATION DATA

Tyrrell, Bernard, 1933–
Christotherapy: healing through enlightenment
"A Crossroad book."
1. Faith-cure.   I.   Title.
BT732.5.T93   615'.852   74-31344
ISBN 0-8164-0278-7

DEDICATION

To my Father
Ben J. Tyrrell
Who in his 77th year
teaches me what a youthful
quality wisdom really is

May 10, 1974

Contents

Preface

Christotherapy: Healing Through Enlightenment is a book with multiple aims. To the sufferer who *truly* seeks healing it suggests a path to wholeness. To the seeker of meaning and direction in life it presents a concrete process of existential diagnosis and discernment. To spiritual directors, therapists, and counselors it offers an initial model of a psychotherapeutic approach rooted and grounded in Christian revelation. To readers interested in the dynamic relationship between psychology and religion it provides a nontechnical sketch of a theology of healing which focuses attention on Jesus Christ as healer of the wounded psyche and spirit of man through the saving light of the meaning and value he incarnates and reveals.

The reader of a book on the dynamics of healing and integration must ultimately test the authenticity of the proposed method through lived experience and vital personal engagement. As St. Paul urges in the first epistle to the Thessalonians: "Test everything; hold fast what is good" (1 Thessalonians 5:21, RSV). Yet, it is perhaps not unfair on the part of the potential reader to ask of the proponent of a dynamic healing therapy what his credentials are for proposing a way of healing through enlightenment.

Happily, I believe that I can attest that, whatever the ultimate judgment of the adequacy or inadequacy of this work may be, at least it is the fruit of personal experience of the type that involves a "shaking of the foundations" and is not the facile product of the uninvolved "armchair theologian."

If I may be somewhat autobiographical, I am a Jesuit priest and a professor of philosophy and religious studies with a doctorate in philosophy. In the late sixties, a few years following my ordination, I had in many ways succumbed to the upheaval and distress that troubled so many of my peer group. The pilgrim of Dante's *Inferno* who in midlife found himself in a dark forest without a pathway well symbolizes the state of my psyche at this critical time.

Despite the darkness of my wilderness situation, I was graced during this period with the opportunity of hearing Bernard Lonergan deliver a series of lectures at Boston College on the meaning of moral and religious conversion. Lonergan emphasized the need for the theologian to be himself an authentic, converted individual as a prerequisite for a truly effective engagement in the theological enterprise. Although thoroughly convinced that Lonergan was correct, I was profoundly pained by the sharp awareness of the gap between the ideal Lonergan proposed and my own confused and anguished state of mind and heart. In the terms of Dr. Kazimierz Dabrowski, I was at a point where the type of integration of living patterns I had previously developed in order to come to grips with life was no longer viable and a certain "positive disintegration" had to take place so that a new and higher integration could occur.

During this period of disintegration my friend Henri Nouwen suggested to me that New York psychiatrist Dr. Thomas Hora might well prove to be the guide I was seeking to lead me out of the dark woods of psychic turmoil and anguish in which I found myself entrapped. As it turned out this was one of the best recommendations I have ever received.

My very first encounter with Dr. Hora was for me a "mind-blowing" experience in the most vital and existential sense of this current popular expression. Dr. Hora spoke to me in some such words as the following: "How ironical it is that you, a Jesuit priest and theologian, should come to a psychiatrist seeking healing. If a religion is truly authentic and if you are a true seeker of life and light through that religion, then it should be the source of healing and wholeness for you on all the levels of your being—the psychic and somatic as well as the moral and spiritual." This statement stunned me because up to that point I had been quite convinced that psychiatry and religion had little or nothing in common and that to try to bring the two together was like the proverbial attempt to mix oil and water.

For some time I was highly skeptical of Dr. Hora's whole approach and I resisted him on point after point. I began, however, to read widely in existential psychotherapy, and the realization grew that authentic religion could and should exercise a healing and integrating influence on the whole person. More importantly, however, following the example of Dr. Hora, I began to meditate on the Scriptures with an inward eye open to the healing meanings and values present in the actions and teachings of Christ. Gradually through the practice of what I now refer to as "the prayerful process of mind-fasting and spirit-feasting," I came to verify for myself that Jesus Christ is truly healer of the wounded psyche of man and that gifts of healing through enlightenment are available to all those who truly seek wholeness and holiness and do so perseveringly.

Besides the influence of my psychiatrist, a four-month residence which I had at Guest House in Rochester, Minnesota, was crucial for my own advance in the healing-through-enlightenment process and my own personal testing and working out of the principles and existential techniques of Christotherapy as I develop them in the present book. It was in the "climate of love" and Spirit-filled tranquillity of Guest House that I was given the inner light to understand a key disharmony in my existence. Once I had existentially diagnosed the meaning of this massive disharmony and had begun to acknowledge and accept the implications of this diagnosis, a radical step forward in my own process of healing and integration took place. I also grew considerably in my God-given existential understanding of the great gulf which exists between the inauthentic and authentic modes-of-being-in-the-world, or what I refer to respectively in the present book as the "gates of hell" and the "gates of paradise." Most importantly, the truth that Christ is healer of the wounded psyche and spirit of man through the power of the meaning and value he incarnates became overwhelmingly clear and manifest to me.

It is now almost five years since my first encounter with Dr. Hora and my experience has been that of a gradual ascension of the "spiral of transcendence," or the healing-through-enlightenment process. I cannot say that there have been no dark periods during this time but there has been growth, and today I experience a serenity, a deep-set joy and an inner calm which I have not known previously. I must at once add, however, that I do not claim to have "arrived." In the words of Robert Frost, "I have promises to keep and miles to go before I sleep." I am still only beginning the awesome ascent of the Mountain. I am, moreover, acutely aware of the fact that "the man who thinks he is safe must be careful that he does not fall" (1 Corinthians 10:12).[1]

There is a precarious quality about the conversion process, and reversal—even radical reversal—is always a possibility. We are, however, commanded to hope and forbidden to despair. Moreover, the best way to assure one's own growth in the healing process is to share the fruits of one's own experience of God's graciousness with others. It is the deep calling of everyone who is healed to become an instrument through which God may do his healing work in others. It is then in the light of the hope I experience and the desire to share whatever gifts of healing I have received that I write the present book.

It is imperative for me to add at this point that in my manuscript as I originally presented it to the publisher there was no mention of my own personal pilgrimage out of the "dark forest" toward healing and enlightenment. I had felt that it would suffice simply to present my notion of Christotherapy and its techniques, and leave it up to the reader to test it in terms of her or his own personal performance. I initially judged that a personal testimony, such as the one I have just presented, would be unnecessary and perhaps even obtrusive. I was and am still quite aware of the fact that I am only a relative beginner and pilgrim in the ways of enlightenment and that it would be absolutely false to claim any sort of guru status. At the urging of the publisher, however, and after some deep soul-searching and consultation with friends whose spiritual insights I respect, I decided that it would probably be best to indicate at least briefly that, however inadequate my notion of Christotherapy and its techniques might be, at least it is borne out of the crucible of personal experience and testing and is not just the product of abstract theological reasoning.

There is no need, I believe, to delay the reader of the preface with a lengthy exposition of what Christotherapy is all about. The book speaks for itself in simple terms. Suffice it to say here that the book is an attempt to work out in a practical, pastoral fashion certain key elements and techniques of an authentic Christian psychotherapy.

In the development of Christotherapy I utilize key therapeutic insights of Thomas Hora, William Glasser, Viktor

Frankl, Kazimierz Dabrowski, and others as aids for uncovering psychotherapeutic elements and techniques at least implicitly operative in Christian revelation. Thus, just as modern developments of the notions of history and evolution have aided us in our understanding of salvation history and of the development of doctrine within Scripture and in the Christian Church, so contemporary psychotherapeutic insights help us to unveil or make explicit those dynamic psychological healing meanings, values, and techniques which were at least implicitly present in revelation from the beginning.

Clearly, two principal foundation stones in the edifice of Christotherapy are the works of the philosopher-theologian Bernard Lonergan, and the writings and personal comments of Thomas Hora. I must at once add, however, that just as Lonergan is not to be blamed for the application of certain of his insights which I make in Christotherapy, so neither is Hora to be looked upon as being responsible for the precise notion of Christotherapy as I develop it. Indeed, there are fundamental differences between Dr. Hora and myself in our respective understanding of the nature of the self and of God, of Jesus Christ and the incarnation, of ecclesial Christianity, and of other important issues. Consequently, it would be a disservice to him and a misreading of my own position to presume that my views are simply an echo of his. Christotherapy as I develop it in the present book is the product of my own peculiar synthesis of a wide-ranging variety of highly idiosyncratic viewpoints and lengthy reflections on my personal psychological and religious experiences. At its roots, however, I do believe that Christotherapy is simply a contemporary expression of the perennial stress in the Christian tradition on Christ as *the physician* and healer of the whole person. All I have done is to focus attention on the psychotherapeutic dimension of the healing Event that is Jesus Christ.

As regards the concrete approach in the present book it is clear that I am influenced by my own Catholic Christian horizon and background. I have made a major effort, however, to be as nontechnical and ecumenical as possible in my approach and expression without betraying the distinctive features of my own particular religious convictions and commitment. Obviously, each Christian ecclesial tradition differs somewhat in its understanding and expression of the healing implications of the Christ-event. It is my hope, however, that the individual reader will, where necessary, adapt what I express in the peculiar terms of my own religious horizon to his or her own particular religious situation. To me, a Catholic, it seems that Protestant Christianity has been far ahead of Catholicism in gaining insight into the psychotherapeutic dimension of the Christ-event. Once I became interested I discovered that Protestant authors far outnumbered Catholics in this vital area. I have consequently been profoundly influenced in my working out of the notion of Christotherapy by various Protestant writers in the area of psychotherapy and religion.

Before concluding this preface I would like to express a few cautions which may prove helpful for a proper reading and understanding of the book.

First, this book is the final product of a number of drafts. In each redrafting there was an attempt at greater simplification. There is consequently a deceptive simplicity about the book which could mislead the reader and end in misunderstanding. The book is intended for meditation and reflection. A quick and summary reading can easily harm rather than help and heal.

Second, I would warn the reader not to begin this book with a preconceived notion of precisely what it is about. It is not a book on faith healing. It is not a book on Pentecostalism. It is not a "how to do it" book in psychology. It is not a meditation manual. It is not a series of spiritual Yoga exercises. It is true that this book may very well prove of importance and relevance to readers interested in any of these areas. But to identify the book from the start with any one of these areas is to do everything one can to block the occurrence of an authentic insight into what Christotherapy is really all about.

Third, in the appendix of this book there are two sections entitled respectively "The Good News of Healing" and "Healing Signs in the Church." Originally I had intended these sections to be the first two chapters of the book. I decided, however, that even though these sections are vitally important for a rounded and foundationally grounded understanding of Christotherapy, it would be best to begin the book immediately with the discussion of Christotherapy itself and to put the scriptural and historical sections on healing at the end of the book. The basic importance of these two sections is that they bring out clearly the fact that the notion of healing through enlightenment is not a recent theological "bright idea" but is clearly grounded in Scripture and Christian tradition. I also believe that these two sections are especially fruitful for an understanding of Jesus Christ as healing-meaning and value both in his lifetime and as he continues to be present in his Church through charismatic and sacramental activities.

Fourth, although I deliberately refrain in the present book from the employment of scholarly apparatus and technical expression, this should not be taken to imply that I do not consider it important to treat Christotherapy in a critical fashion. In fact, in June 1974 at a Lonergan Symposium in Boston I presented a paper entitled "On the Possibility and Desirability of a Christian Psychotherapy." In this paper I did attempt to articulate the notion of Christotherapy in a critical manner. I judged it best, however, in the present book to present Christotherapy in a direct, pastoral fashion which would be helpful to the general reader.

Fifth, in somewhat the same vein as the preceding comment, to the Scripture scholar who might chance to read this book, I should indicate that at times I make use of scriptural references in an applied, nonliteral fashion for inspirational purposes. This should not be taken, however, to imply that I am a devotee of fundamentalism. I am quite convinced that the basic thrust of my notion of Christotherapy is in profound accord with Scripture, even though in the present book I have not attempted to demonstrate this in the rigorous fashion the professional exegete might prefer.

In conclusion I would like to express special thanks to a number of people for their aid in one way or other in the completion of the present book.

Clearly, to Thomas Hora and Bernard Lonergan, I am indebted in more ways than I could ever explain. Likewise, I owe a very special debt of gratitude to Robert Egan, Peter Ely, and William Ryan, all fellow Jesuits, who through their friendship and advice have been a constant source of encouragement and help to me. Likewise, I am immensely grateful to Lincoln Reinhardt, my counselor at Guest House, who mediated God's love to me in a very special fashion. I am also deeply indebted to José Ingojo, who undertook the laborious task of transforming my initial draft into more readable prose. Without his long labor and constant encouragement the manuscript would still be uncompleted. Likewise, for the work they did on my manuscript, I would like to thank Sister Cecilia Wilms, Chris Gjording, Charles Keenan, John Navone, Patty O'Connell, and Phyllis Pobst.

Lastly, I would like to express most special thanks to the

many students at Gonzaga University, Spokane, Washington, to whom I have had the privilege of teaching the course
entitled "Healing through Enlightenment" in the past three
years. In semester after semester large classes have re-
sponded enthusiastically. Most importantly and significantly, many students have told me of the transforming
effect that the practice of the principles of Christotherapy
has had on their lives. It is this spontaneous, powerful response on the part of the young—and many who are not so
young—which above all indicates to me that Christ is indeed the living, ever-present source of those healing meanings and values which bring wholeness to the wounded
psyche and spirit of man.

NOTES

1. Scriptural citations in this work are from the Jerusalem Bible unless
indicated otherwise.

I

Christotherapy: Healing through the Christ Meaning

THE THEME OF THIS BOOK is healing through enlightenment and specifically healing through the light and value that are revealed in Christ. I have coined the term "Christotherapy" to designate the particular approach to Christ the Healer developed in this work. Literally Christotherapy means the therapy or healing that comes through Christ. In the broad sense Christotherapy obviously includes the entire saving work of Christ in all of its aspects. But the specific meaning which I intend for Christotherapy is the healing through enlightenment that Christ offers as the truth-value that sets us free.

The Gospel of John stresses that Christ is the true light which enlightens everyone who comes into the world. John's Gospel likewise emphasizes that Christ is the way and the life and the truth and that, as the truth, Jesus sets us free from our bondage. Christotherapy, accordingly, places its primary stress on the healing power of the Christ-meaning and the Christ-value. Thus, just as Viktor Frankl's logotherapy urges that the discovery of meaning and value in life can heal certain "neuroses" so, analogously, Christotherapy emphasizes that a God-given understanding of the

Christotherapy

Christ-meaning and a response to the Christ-value in one or other of its many aspects can effect the healing not only of the spirit but of the wounded psyche and at times the body as well. Christotherapy primarily focuses attention on the wholeness, holiness, and fullness of life which come to the individual through a lived understanding of the Christ-meaning and a loving response to the Christ-value.

What is perhaps most distinctive about Christotherapy is that it puts great stress on the healing power of meaning and above all on the Christ-meaning. For Christotherapy a most important prayer is: "Lord, that I may understand." The term "enlightenment" best expresses the fruitful type of understanding which is the concern of Christotherapy because enlightenment implies a knowledge that is *received*, and not just any knowledge but a knowledge that is life-giving and full of value.

Christotherapy concerns itself with the freeing of men and women from all forms of servitude but it occupies itself in a very special way with the overcoming of ignorance and, in particular, "existential ignorance." Christotherapy defines existential ignorance as a mere passive ignorance or as an active ignoring of those meanings and values which are essential for the achievement, or rather active reception, of the gifts of wholeness and enlightened holiness. Most certainly, Christotherapy has as one of its most vital concerns the overcoming of a sinful state of mind and heart through repentance and conversion. But Christotherapy sees existential ignorance as one of the primary effects of the original and personal sinfulness of mankind and as one of the chief obstacles to growth in wholeness and enlightened holiness.

Christotherapy focuses attention on the overcoming of ignorance and the active reception of the gift of enlightened holiness because these elements are often enough not given sufficient attention in books on spirituality and psychology written within a Christian framework. Christotherapy also emphasizes that sin—both original and personal—is at the root of all human difficulties; for sin, too, as a central reality in human life, has been downplayed and even ignored by many contemporary writers. Happily, however, Karl Menninger has recently astounded the world of psychiatry by asking a radical question: "Whatever became of sin?"

In regard to the issue of "enlightened holiness" Christotherapy recognizes that the presence of holiness in an individual does not necessarily mean that the saint in question has transcended all forms of existential ignorance. The history of the Christian religion is filled with examples of women and men who were truly saints but, unfortunately, remained scarred with varying degrees of existential ignorance. Dr. Josef Goldbrunner speaks out clearly against such aspects of otherwise saintly lives:

There are unhealthy features in the faces of the saints which are not the expression of true human suffering. We read of illnesses which are not necessary, illnesses of the body and soul which represent untruth, since they are caused by false attitudes, by false ways of life, by a false conduct of life, not in accordance with the laws of nature nor with the true relationship between the natural and the supernatural. These "illegitimate illnesses" are contrary to nature. But such mutilations of life, physical and spiritual, have become so identified with the very notion of holiness that one almost has to smile, when calling a man a saint, as if to apologize for his manifest oddity.[1]

Goldbrunner's point is that good will, even heroic good will and holiness, do not necessarily imply the absence of untruth and false attitudes. Christotherapy, accordingly, emphasizes that Christ did not come simply to make us holy but to make us whole and to fill us with the light of truth which frees us from all our diseases, existential ignorance included. Further, although I make a certain distinction between holiness and enlightened holiness, I do not mean to imply that they are ever completely separated. The gifts of a deep love and faith must be present in any saint and the indwelling of these gifts in a human heart indicates a profound state of enlightenment.

Christotherapy and the God-Meaning

To understand in its deeper implications the stress of Christotherapy on Christ's role as healer through the meaning and value he incarnates, it is necessary to envisage God in the context of meaning. From the viewpoint of Christotherapy, God is meaning itself and the meaning which underpins and ultimately grounds all limited meanings. God, in the transcendent richness of his meaning, is a brightness too rich for our limited understanding ever to comprehend. Though God is the explanation of all, there is no finite understanding which will ever succeed in plumbing the depths of the transcendent mystery that is God. God is infinite understanding and infinite love, such that all the creatures which proceed from him bear the mark of his intelligence and love. God alone is the absolute, the transcendent one who creates and sustains all things; he is dependent on nothing and yet is more intimately present to his creation than it is to itself, than we are to ourselves. God is wisdom and this wisdom is "unique, manifold, subtle"; she is "active, incisive, unsullied, / lucid, invulnerable, benevolent, sharp"; this wisdom that is God is "irresistible, beneficent, loving to man, / steadfast, dependable, unperturbed, / almighty, all-surveying, / penetrating all intelligent, pure / and most subtle spirits" (Wisdom 7:22-23). Scripture tells us that "over Wisdom evil can never triumph." The wisdom that is God "deploys her strength from one end of the earth to the other, / ordering all things for good" (Wisdom 7:30-8:1).

The quest of the human spirit for a loving meaning in all things is rooted in the fact that God is wisdom itself and loving meaning itself, and that all things are pervaded with the subtle influence that is the very love and wisdom of God himself. In poetic words cited by Paul: "It is in him that we live, and move, and exist" (Acts 17:28).

The deepest meaning of God, however, goes beyond the fact that he is infinite love and wisdom itself and the milieu which sustains us and in which we abide. The richest word about God revealed to his children is that he is three persons—Father, Son, and Spirit—who together in their common nature share in the same infinitely rapturous act of joy-filled understanding and love. As Bernard Lonergan has so beautifully expressed it: "The three Persons are the perfect community, not two in one flesh, but three subjects of a single, dynamic, existential consciousness."[2] This wondrous, ineffable mystery of God as Trinity is the most profound meaning of God and, as shall be developed more at length later, it is the *Beatific Participation* in the inner life of the Triune God that is the ultimate bliss and consummation of the enlightenment process.

Christ the Healing Light

God has not been silent in the presence of his creation but has spoken out and continues to speak out in a rich variety of ways. In nature God speaks his cosmic words to his daughters and sons: "The heavens declare the glory of God, / the vault of heaven proclaims his handiwork" (Psalm 19:1). In man's own exercise of intelligent and loving activities God silently reveals something about his own being as love-intelligence. Through certain chosen individuals God declares his prophetic word to his children. But it is in

Christ, the very Word of God made flesh, that God speaks his definitive and lasting word and reveals the deepest secret and mysteries of his own inner life.

In the epistle to the Hebrews it is written that "in our own time, the last days, he has spoken to us through his Son, the Son that he has appointed to inherit everything and through whom he made everything there is" (Hebrews 1:2-3). Christ is described as "the radiant light of God's glory and the perfect copy of his nature" (Hebrews 1:3), and the Gospel of John says that he is "the Way, the Truth, and the Life" (John 14:6). Thomas Aquinas in the prologue of Part III of the *Summa Theologica* says that Jesus our saviour showed us in himself the way of truth through which we might reach eternal life. Thus, in the light of the scriptural stress on Christ as truth, Christotherapy concerns itself profoundly with the healing available to us in Christ as the way and as the "light of the world" (John 8:12).

In reflecting on Christ as healing light it is important to stress that Jesus brings salvation to us not only through his atoning death and resurrection but also—in a sense more fundamentally—through his very being what he is. Christ is light and it is natural for light to dispel darkness. Christ is truth and it is of the very essence of truth's dynamic to remove ignorance. Christ is life and life is inimical to disease and disharmony in all of its forms.

In an address to fellow psychiatrists Thomas Hora, in a comment most unusual for a man engaged in psychotherapy, indirectly sheds light on the healing that Christ brings to mankind through his very existence as light and truth:

In the last analysis, we may arrive at the momentous discovery that what we as psychotherapists say has little or no effect (unless at times detrimental), and what really matters is *what we are*. Thus we come back to a Taoist insight of over 2000 years ago pronounced by that Chinese sage Lao-Tzu: "The way to do is to be."[3]

Hora here maintains as a principle that only in terms of what a person is, is his doing ultimately of any significance. In this same light, what Christ was and is—truth, light, life, way, love—gives his words and deeds their fundamental meaning and their definitive healing and enlightening power. Whatever Jesus did flowed from what he was and is—the Word made flesh, "the same today as he was yesterday and as he will be for ever" (Hebrews 13: 8-9).

Just as one stresses Christ's divine participation in the truth that is God as the primal source of meaning in all that he said and did, so also one must emphasize that it is precisely in his incarnation as a man like us that the meaning which he incarnates achieves its deep significance for us. It was "for us men and for our salvation" that the Word was made flesh and consequently there is no aspect of God's self-revelation in Christ that does not tell us something existentially important about ourselves. Karl Rahner in his theological writings constantly emphasizes that every truth of revelation has profound anthropological implications. Add to this that every aspect of God's self-revelation in Christ has a healing and enlightening meaning and value for the lives of men and women. More concretely, this means that everything Christ said and did contained a healing meaning and value for mankind and those who truly seek healing through enlightenment should pray that their eyes may be opened so that they may discern the healing meanings operative for them in every dimension of the Christ-event.

Unfortunately, many Christians look to Christ's teachings simply to acquire a notional knowledge about God or at best to learn what commandments and moral precepts they must obey if they are to be saved. These Christians fail to take Christ seriously as loving, healing truth and to seek in Christ's words and actions the unveiling of those existential life-giving meanings and values which will heal them of their diseases—mental, emotional, and physical as well as spiritual—and fill them in a certain true fashion even in this life with the dawning light of the resurrection.

Key Forms of Christian Enlightenment

Healing and enlightenment are two words which are very rich in denotation and connotation. In the strict denotative sense, healing is a term that refers to the overcoming of the negative factor, the diseased element in the person, and the restoration of wholeness. Enlightenment is a word that denotes the attainment of spiritual insight, growth in understanding.

Classical Christian theology saw man as in need of "healing grace" and "elevating or transforming grace." The healing-through-enlightenment process is looked upon as a process that effects healing and brings about ever higher levels of existential wholeness and holiness in the person through the transforming power of Christ as light and life incarnate. In the perspective of Christian theology, the human person is in need of the healing grace of God in order to be freed from the bondage of sin and its effects; likewise, men and women are capable of becoming, through the free gift of God's gracious love in Christ, sons or daughters of God and sharing in the divine nature (2 Peter 1:4). Christotherapy concerns itself with the process of healing through enlightenment whereby the true seekers of salvation are healed of their wounds and gradually divinized and transformed into the glorious likeness of Christ, beloved Son of the Father.

Before analyzing certain key forms of enlightenment I should make it clear that I speak of *Christian* enlightenment, even though the phenomenon of enlightenment is in no way restricted to explicitly Christian contexts. There is, for example, the whole area of Buddhist and Zen enlightenment. Likewise, there is the rich zone of so-called "naturalist" enlightenment—the enlightenment of the nature poets, of Wordsworth, Coleridge, Whitman, etc. As a Christian theologian, of course, I believe that it is ultimately through Christ that all healing through enlightenment comes; but I also believe that in a mysterious fashion Christ's healing power is at work in all great religions and in holy men and women of all ages—

for Christ plays in ten thousand places
Lovely in limbs, and lovely in eyes not his
to the Father through the features of men's faces —[4]

and that the gift of God's love and the fruits of the Spirit may be discerned in Buddhists, Hindus, etc., as well as in Christians, and even that Christians have much to learn about enlightenment from these other great world religions. I largely prescind, however, in this book from a discussion of enlightenment as it occurs in contexts which are not explicitly Christian because not every issue can be handled in a short book and because there is complexity enough involved in analyzing the various forms and stages of explicit Christian enlightenment.

In the remainder of this chapter I will concentrate on four principal forms of enlightenment and on four basic attitudes which I think should characterize the individual who seeks to cooperate with Christ as he carries out his work of healing through enlightenment within the human heart. The four forms of healing through enlightenment are: existential diagnosis; existential discernment; conversion; and mysticism. The four attitudes of heart are: humbleness of heart; listening; "letting-be"; and *wu wei*. I should note that Christotherapy is not something utterly different from the types of enlightenment and attitudes of heart just mentioned. Rather, Christotherapy is a specific, formal articulation of the different ways in which healing and fullness of life can come through a lived understanding of and participation in the Christ-meaning and value. Thus, just as logotherapy serves to remind us in a formal, articulate fashion that the discovery of meaning and value in life can bring healing, so Christotherapy as a psychotheological type of reflection hopes to indicate how there is healing power enough in the Christ-meaning to free an individual from all of his diseases and make him holy and whole. Christotherapy then is not something entirely separate from the types of enlightenment and attitudes of the heart that foster healing through enlightenment. Rather, just as theology is born of religious experience and is a reflection on it, so Christotherapy is born of the concrete healing-through-enlightenment process and is an effort to articulate and thematize it in certain of its points.

Existential Diagnosis: A First Form of Christian Enlightenment

Existential diagnosis involves the discovery or understanding of the meaning of the negative factors in one's life, the diseases and disharmonies which one experiences. Lonergan provides grounds for this preliminary form of enlightenment when he stresses in his *Method in Theology* that it is much better to acknowledge our feelings regardless of how objectionable they are rather than ignore them. In taking cognizance of our feelings we are better able to know ourselves and understand and correct those things in us which are undesirable.[5] Hora also points out that it is necessary to listen to the " 'Silent Voice' of Existence," to understand the "silent messages," inherent in symptoms. Hora considers this a condition for even the possibility of healing. Lonergan and Hora are both in their own way saying that the understanding of one's actual mode of existence-in-the-world is a preliminary moment in the process that moves toward the attainment of full enlightenment. As Hora puts it in speaking of the role of the true healer:

The task of the physician is to help the patient understand the language of existence whether it speaks from his body, his mind, or his destiny. Existence speaks from the body *via* the symptoms, from the mind *via* the mental condition; and from destiny *via* the unfolding of personal history. Authentic existence requires man to be in constant communion with and in mindfulness of the silent voice of his existential conscience. Such mindfulness and communion are the basis of enlightened self-understanding.[6]

Christotherapy, then, is concerned both with healing and enlightenment. It is the positive rather than the negative pole which enjoys central attention. The point may be better understood by contrasting the Freudian with the Third Force approach to psychology exemplified by Abraham Maslow and Carl Rogers. Freud's concern was with the negative, diseased aspects of man. Maslow, however, was interested in man as psychologically healthy and mature. He said that Freud had supplied the sick half of psychology and it was his task to provide the healthy half. Christotherapy, in contradistinction to Freud's stress, is fundamentally bipolar in its interest; it concerns itself with both sickness and health, weakness and strength, the negative and the positive in man. Christotherapy assigns a primacy to the positive pole in the healing and enlightening process, yet it recognizes that suffering, existential ignorance, sickness, and death are "facts" in man's present historical situation, and that it is impossible to move toward the positive without also coming to grips with the negative. Thus, Christ not only occupied himself with revealing to man the authentic way to live and be existentially fulfilled in the world; he also spent time casting out devils. Christ clearly understood that it is never enough just to exorcise a devil; the demonic power must be replaced by a power for good and an inward enlightenment in the individual. Otherwise, as Christ indicated, the last stage of the individual may be worse than the beginning.

When an unclean spirit goes out of a man it wanders through waterless country looking for a place to rest, and cannot find one. Then it says, "I will return to the home I came from." But on arrival, finding it unoccupied, swept and tidied, it then goes off and collects seven other spirits more evil than itself, and they go in and set up house there, so that the man ends up by being worse than he was before.

Matthew 12:43-45

Christotherapy concerns itself with the casting out of all types of "devils"; but it realizes that the essential thing is the possession of an inward eye full of light.

This has not been an exhaustive discussion of existential diagnosis and its role in Christotherapy. Existential diagnosis will be discussed more fully in Chapter IV, "Mind-Fasting and Spirit-Feasting."

Existential Discernment of God's Positive Will: A Second Form of Christian Enlightenment

The second form of enlightenment is a positive complement to the first. It consists in understanding the positive directives and calls which God gives to us as we work out our salvation. To describe this form of enlightenment in the terms of Paul, it is a matter of discovering the "will of God" and of knowing "what is good, what it is that God wants, what is the perfect thing to do" (Romans 12:2).

Existential discernment of God's will, like existential diagnosis, finds a certain parallel in Ignatius Loyola's "discernment of spirits" as developed in his *Spiritual Exercises.* Ignatius sets up various rules for discerning which desires, thoughts, etc., are inspired by God and which are not. In Ignatius' view it is essential that one discover what thoughts are the result of God's inspiration and providential guidance and then follow out resolutely the summons or call or concrete will of God for us when it is discovered. Existential discernment, then, is a process that is similar to Ignatian discernment, and like Ignatian discernment is ultimately rooted in the revealed word of God. Holy Scripture is filled with prayers on the part of individuals for an understanding of what God wants of them, and existential discernment is simply a formal expression of this basic dimension of Christian experience. This brief explication of existential discernment, will be expanded upon in relation to spirit-feasting in Chapter IV.

Religious Conversion:
Third Form of Christian Enlightenment

Religious conversion is the central form of Christian enlightenment. The first two types, or forms, of Christian enlightenment are ordered toward the occurrence of, or growth in, religious conversion, and the fourth form— mysticism—is a crowning moment in the realization of the fruits of conversion.

Religious conversion is a multidimensional process. In the Hebrew and New Testaments it means a change of mind and heart, a turning from sin, from idols, from an evil way. Repentance is a key element in the conversion process; in repenting, sorrow for sin is expressed; there is a rejection of false values, attitudes, habits, and a personal commitment in love and fidelity to God. Conversion is the work of God. God alone blots out our transgressions and gives us a new mind and heart full of righteousness, love, and truth.

According to Bernard Lonergan religious conversion consists in the gift of God's love flooding one's heart. The knowledge born of that experience he calls "faith" or the "eye of love."[7] Religious conversion and every inner illumination and strengthening that lead to its occurrence and development are the free gifts of God and cannot be merited. Though religious conversion is first and most radically the gracious operation of God in transforming our hearts, its effectiveness in moving us toward a full and complete state of enlightenment requires free cooperation. Also, religious conversion, though an intensely personal affair, is not private in a solitary sense. Lonergan points out that conversion can happen to many and they can form a community to sustain each other in their self-transformation and in working out the practical implications of their lives. Lonergan emphasizes the importance of the existence of a milieu, or climate, of love in which the process of religious conversion may be deepened and become ever more fruitful. In the case of religious conversion that is explicitly Christian, belief in Christ as the Word made flesh and in his unique saving deeds is operative, and growth in conversion involves an ever deeper existential understanding of the mystery of Christ and a transformation into his image.

The core transformative moment of religious conversion is God's gift of his love or of a "new heart" (Ezekiel 18:31). Thus, in the account of Jeremiah, Yahweh says: "I will give them a heart to acknowledge that I am Yahweh. They shall be my people and I shall be their God, for they will return to me with all their heart" (Jeremiah 24:7). Ezekiel, moreover, expresses the very core of the conversion process when he refers to Yahweh as saying: "I will give them a single heart and I will put a new spirit in them; I will remove the heart of stone from their bodies and give them a heart of flesh instead" (Ezekiel 11:18-19; cf. 36:26). To grasp these texts one must recall that in the Hebrew understanding, heart does not mean simply or primarily the center of emotion or affection, but signifies the center of intelligence and love; it is the source of all our thoughts, desires, and deeds. For Yahweh to give us a new heart means that he pours forth into us a new love and a new knowledge. The Hebrew Testament view of the intercommunion of love and knowledge in religious conversion is well summed up in Hosea where, in speaking of the need for conversion, he puts these words on Yahweh's lips: "What I want is love, not sacrifice; knowledge of God, not holocaust" (Hosea 6:6). Knowledge and love are gifts from God.

In the New Testament writings, especially in the epistles of Paul and the Gospel and epistles of John, the intercommunion of knowledge and love in the conversion process is strongly emphasized. Paul expresses the key moment of religious conversion: "The love of God has been poured into our hearts by the Holy Spirit which has been given to us" (Romans 5:5). For Paul, however, the possession of the gift of God's love also involves a knowledge. Thus, he prays for the Ephesians that

Christ may live in your hearts through faith, and then, planted in love and built on love, you will with all the saints have strength to grasp the breadth and the length, the height and the depth; until, knowing the love of Christ, which is beyond all knowledge, you are filled with the utter fullness of God.

Ephesians 3:17-19

For Paul knowledge and love merge into one in their perfection. Knowing requires choosing and loving without reservation. In John the heart of the conversion process is a love that fructifies in knowledge and a knowledge that leads to ever deeper love. John indicates that it is eternal life to know the Father and his Son (John 17:3). This knowing is a loving knowing. "Everyone who loves is begotten by God and knows God. / Anyone who fails to love can never have known God, / because God is love" (1 John 4:7-8). For John to love God is to know God. As John McKenzie remarks: "In John knowledge and love grow together, so that it is difficult to say whether the love is the fruit of knowledge or knowledge is the fruit of love."[8]

Mysticism: A Fourth Form of Christian Enlightenment

Spiritual writers throughout the centuries in their treatises on prayer have stressed that as individuals grow in their knowledge and love of God, their prayer tends to become more simple. Fewer words are used, less thinking goes on, and prayer becomes more and more a matter of simply abiding quietly in the loving presence of God. There is, then, in the process of growth in prayer a movement from the activities of reflecting, meditating, etc., toward a certain dynamic loving quiescence, a creative stillness, a simple letting God be God as he abides within one's heart.

Lonergan in discussing various types of religious consciousness indicates that the beginning of religious development is ascetical in its impetus and mystical in its culmination. As growth occurs there takes place a gradual shift from an authentic exercise of asceticism and self-discipline toward a self-surrender to the action of God in one's heart. It is in the gift of God's love that both the genuinely ascetical and the mystical differentiations of religious consciousness have their ground. In the transformation process, as we yield more and more to God operative within us, we have an ever deepening *experience* of the loving presence of God within our hearts. Gradually, there is a withdrawal from the world of images and constructs into an all-embracing self-surrender to God's gift of his love. Lonergan is using classical mystical terminology when he speaks of the shift in states of consciousness as a certain withdrawal into a cloud of unknowing. In this mystical state one belongs to God, one gives oneself to God through a peaceful surrender to his initiative. There are manifold forms of mysticism but the main component of all of them is the silent and all-absorbing self-surrender in response to God's gift of his love. In this state there is a heightened awareness or experience of the gift of God's love present within the heart, and a peaceful abiding in the experience of the love of God dwelling within one.

Mysticism in its fundamental form—and I am not speaking here of visions, raptures, etc.—is the crowning moment in the enlightenment process. It is not something extraordinary and reserved for the chosen few but is an ordinary stage in the process of Christian maturation. Christian mysticism is simply the intensification of the ordinary Christian life, a deepening of the faith and love possessed by every true Christian. Mystics are believers who love God so intensely that the love takes on a highly experiential character. This description of Christian mysticism is consistent with a direction commonly taken by writers on mysticism: Evelyn Underhill, Thomas Merton, William Johnston, to name a few. There are extraordinary forms of mysticism not offered to all; but the type of mysticism spoken of here is the natural fruit of a life of faith and love lived to the full.

Mysticism is the highest state of enlightenment and hence is less often experienced by many individuals than are the first three forms of Christian enlightenment. Mysticism is the highest goal of healing and enlightenment attainable in life.

It must be noted that my division of the forms of enlightenment could be considered somewhat arbitrary. I have chosen these four divisions—existential diagnosis, existential discernment, religious conversion, and mysticism—because they are adequate for my purposes. It should also be noted that the four forms of Christian enlightenment are interrelated and not mutually exclusive. Thus mystics on occasion may still have to discern the meaning of certain disharmonies in their existence and they must constantly discern in their everyday affairs the direction God wishes them to follow. And similarly the less perfect occasionally taste God as the sweet presence abiding within them and they are in constant need of discernment of God's will for them and growth in the knowledge of Christ. Finally, existential diagnosis and discernment have as their aim the occurrence of, or growth in, religious conversion. It might then be legitimately said that in a profound sense all the forms of enlightenment are dimensions of the conversion process.

Man's Role as Cooperator with God in the Process of Healing through Enlightenment

God is the primary agent in the whole process of healing through enlightenment, but the human subject is free to cooperate with God in the process or to fail to cooperate. There are four basic attitudes which I think should characterize the individual who is truly cooperating with God as he carries out his work of healing through enlightenment. These four attitudes, or modes, of response are: humbleness of heart, listening, "letting-be," and *wu wei.*

HUMBLENESS OF HEART

It is a fundamental teaching in both the Hebrew and New Testaments that an attitude of humbleness of heart is an absolute prerequisite for God's effective operation in the human heart. "God opposes the proud but he gives generously to the humble" (James 4:6). The individual who is authentically responsive to God's operation in his heart acknowledges that God alone is Lord and Giver of life; he further confesses that God is the source of every good, holy, and perfect gift (cf. James 1:16-17) and that, as Paul expressed it, "it is God, for his own loving purpose, who puts both the will and the action" (Philippians 2:13) into man. Authentically responsive persons existentially recognize in their hearts that of themselves they are nothing (Galatians 6:3) and can do nothing; they recognize that of themselves they are "mere servants" (Luke 17:10) and that on their own they cannot take one step toward the Source of all healing through enlightenment (John 6:44). Paul indicates very clearly the attitude of humility which should characterize the authentic response to God at work in us when he writes to the Ephesians:

It is by grace that you have been saved, through faith; not by anything of your own, but by a gift from God; not by anything you have done, so that nobody can claim the credit. We are God's work of art, created in Christ Jesus to live the good life as from the beginning he had meant us to live it.

Ephesians 2:8-10

Scripture does not deny that we are called to cooperate freely with God as he works within us, but it stresses throughout that God is the initiator and main actor in the transformation of the human heart, and that even our free cooperation is a gift of God.

Modern men and women are inclined to envisage themselves as the chief architects of their destinies and salvation.

But this is a fundamental illusion and it puts us into conflict with Existence. In this context Hora remarks that in Heidegger's interpretation the Oedipus myth points to man's passion for knowledge as the perennial source of the tragic character of human existence. The tragedy of Oedipus is not a sexual drama but a drama about man's self-righteous striving for knowledge.[9] Hora emphasizes that we must not be self-righteous in our search for knowledge; to know authentically we must be open, humble, receptive, reverential, and not grasping, usurping, intruding. Hora sees the latter approach to knowing as a major block to the occurrence of healing through enlightenment in the individual. His analysis confirms from a certain psychological perspective the scriptural stress on the need for humbleness of heart if we are to be healed. Humility is truth; and the truth is that God is the "God of the humble" (Judith 9:11), just as much in the present age of technology and historical consciousness as he was in the time of the patriarchs, prophets, and apostles. If we now truly seek an inner transformation, an interior healing and enlightenment, we must bow down before the Lord, become as little children and existentially understand that only to little ones does God reveal his healing light.

LISTENING

Throughout Scripture we are exhorted repeatedly to listen. "Whoever will listen, let him listen" (Ezekiel 3:27). "Listen, anyone who has ears" (Matthew 13:9). To listen is to be alert, awake, attentive. It is easy not to listen. Christ speaks of those who have ears and do not hear (Mark 8:18). To hear is not simply a passive act. One hears to the extent that one wants to hear. Hearing involves an active element. Authentic spiritual listening and hearing transcend the categories of passivity and activity. Just as on the physical level of hearing both the existence of longitudinal waves in the atmosphere and ears capable of hearing are required for hearing to occur, on the spiritual level of hearing both God's actual speaking of his word to us and our active hearing of God's word in our mind and heart are required for spiritual hearing to occur. God speaks to us in his cosmic word and in his prophetic word, but above all—and once and for all—in his Christ. The Father's will for us in regard to his Christ is clear: "This is my Son, the Beloved; he enjoys my favor. Listen to him" (Matthew 17:5).

Authentic listening to Christ is that dynamic, active receptivity which leads to the "keeping" of every word that comes forth from Christ. The Virgin Mary provides for us the prototype of the authentic hearer of the word of God and of what happens to one who hears God's word. Thus, at the time of the Annunciation, Mary, in response to the angel's command to "listen" (Luke 1:31), promptly does so and then in reply to the message says, "Let what you have said be done to me" (Luke 1:38). The result is that the very Word of God is made flesh in the womb of the Virgin. It is the calling of every person to be actively receptive to the word which comes forth from the mouth of God and to allow oneself through the interior "hearing" and "keeping" of that word to be healed and enlightened, to be transformed into the image of Christ.

"LETTING-BE"

Hora employs Martin Heidegger's expression "letting-be" to indicate an attitude which he believes is crucial in the process of effective therapy. In my view it is of equal importance in the healing-through-enlightenment process which leads to an ever deeper realization in oneself of the Christ-consciousness. In Hora's understanding "letting-be" is not a matter of quietism or passivity, or of leaving alone.

It is a free, loving allowing of a thing to be what it is so that it can reveal itself in the essence of its being.

Hora believes that "letting-be" expresses an attitude of the highest ethical order because it means relating oneself to the other in an affirmative, loving, perceptive manner. Affirmation of a person's freedom is for Hora an act of love.

From my standpoint it is of the greatest importance to have an attitude of "letting-be" in regard to God. God must be freely allowed by the individual to manifest himself as lover and saviour in the ways and forms he chooses. In true love the lovers freely allow each other to be what they are in their manifestation and expression of love. Existence, or God, freely manifests himself to us, and we, as ones who participate in Love-Intelligence as an image, must freely allow God to be God, light, and saviour for us. Christ stands at the door of the human heart and knocks (Revelation 3:20) and offers to manifest himself; but it is only to as many as receive him, or in other words, to as many as "let him be" light, revealer, and saviour for them, that he imparts the gifts of healing and enlightenment and the power to become daughters and sons of God. Letting-be is far more than an abstract philosophical principle or lyric slogan of contemporary youth's "cultic" approach to love; it is an existential attitude and mode of response of the highest excellence underlying all true love-encounters.

WU WEI

Wu wei is a Taoist expression for the type of action, or better, the actionless action that flows from a life rooted in *Tao*. There are many diverse interpretations of the meaning of *wu wei* and *Tao*, but I have chosen to rely on Huston Smith's understanding of *wu wei*[10] and John Wu's interpretation of *Tao*,[11] as these particular interpretations are most germane to the theme being developed in this chapter.

Wu wei is the chief concern, but it must be understood within the *Tao* context. In John Wu's interpretation of *Tao* as described by the Chinese philosopher Chuang Tzu, *Tao* is absolute; it is the origin and end of everything. *Tao* is creative, directive, and normative. It is present in all things and yet transcends everything. It is infinite, the cause of all changes and the mystery of mysteries. It dwells within us, and through union with it we become children of heaven. In Wu's view, through a special providence of God, Chuang Tzu was able to reach a very profound grasp of the meaning of *Tao* and to discover that the whole universe is pointing to the mystery that is *Tao*. There is a certain striking affinity between *Tao* and the wisdom of the Hebrew Testament. Wu considers the *Tao* to be a pointing to the divine Logos.

Huston Smith joins the concept of *wu wei* to *Tao*. He considers *wu wei* to be the suppleness and simplicity and freedom which flow through us when we yield our private egos and conscious efforts to a power which is not their own. Smith equates this power with *Tao*. So from Smith's view, to practice *wu wei* is to allow the *Tao* to work within one. Smith also translates *wu wei* as "creative quietude." He indicates that *wu wei* is more properly likened to the activity of the truly creative artist who freely allows artistic insights to arise from his subliminal depths, rather than to the craftsman who calculates, works strictly according to sets of rules, etc. *Wu wei* is an openness to the voice of *Tao* within one. This perspective sees man not as a self-enclosed autonomous entity, or in Hora's terminology, as "primary reality." The individual in whom *wu wei* is quietly operative is riding on the unbounded sea of *Tao*. The sea feeds the individual through his subliminal mind. Creative quietude, or the nonaction that is action, is a matter of openness and of being entirely receptive to the guidance of *Tao*.

Wu wei enjoys a close affinity with humility, listening, and letting-be, the three authentic existential modes of response to God described earlier. Just as in the Christian perspective it is God who is radically giver and the human person who is receiver, so in the Taoist view of things it is *Tao* that is primary, and human persons exist authentically to the extent that they let *Tao* work within them. The early Taoists recognized that everything is effortlessly accomplished by the *Tao* and that the most important thing for us is to not interfere and to be receptive to the action of the *Tao*. Hora's belief that all goes well with us to the extent that we remain in accord with Existence or the Love-Intelligence that is the ground of all things is similar to the Taoist stress on receptivity and remaining in harmony with the *Tao*.

Christotherapy is interested in *Tao* and *wu wei* because the Taoist vision enables the seeker of healing through enlightenment to understand the type of response that should be made to Christ—the healing way and light. *Tao* means "way" and Christ is *the* way. Through *wu wei* the individual lets *Tao* work gently and efficaciously within him, and similarly, a *wu wei* type of response to Christ as healing truth enables him to work powerfully within our hearts and to lead us to the point of transformation where we can say: "I live now not with my own life but with the life of Christ who lives in me" (Galatians 2:20).

It is important to try to test and verify in one's own religious experience the quality and validity of humbleness of heart, listening, letting-be, and *wu wei* as responses to God. We must ask ourselves if we experience letting-be as a way of existing in the world. We must ask if we experience the creative quietude that is *wu wei* in our own experience. The way we answer these questions provides an indication of our openness to healing and enlightenment.

NOTES

1. Josef Goldbrunner, *Holiness Is Wholeness* (Notre Dame, Indiana: University of Notre Dame Press, 1964), p. 3.

2. Bernard Lonergan, "The Dehellenization of Dogma," *Theological Studies* 28 (June 1967): 346.

3. Thomas Hora, "Epistemological Aspects of Existence and Psychotherapy," *Journal of Individual Psychology* 15 (November 1959): 173.

4. Gerard Manley Hopkins, *Inversnaid*, lines 28–30.

5. Bernard Lonergan, *Method in Theology* (New York: Seabury Press, 1972), pp. 33-34.

6. Hora, "Epistemological Aspects of Existence and Psychotherapy," p. 168.

7. Lonergan, *Method in Theology*, p. 117.

8. John L. McKenzie, *Dictionary of the Bible* (Milwaukee: Bruce Publishing Company, 1965), p. 487.

9. Hora, "Epistemological Aspects of Existence," p. 170.

10. Huston Smith, *The Religions of Man* (New York: Perennial Library, Harper & Row, 1965), pp. 204–7.

11. John C. H. Wu, *Chinese Humanism and Christian Spirituality* (New York: St. John's University Press, 1965), pp. 53–91.

II

A Dialectic
of Therapies

CHRISTOTHERAPY DOES NOT ARISE from nowhere, without prominent relatives in other approaches to wholeness. The very expression "Christotherapy" is inspired by Viktor Frankl's logotherapy and William Glasser's reality therapy. Christotherapy shares with Dr. Frankl a stress on the healing power of meaning, but looks to Jesus Christ—the Word made flesh—as *the* logotherapist and healer through the meaning he incarnates. Christotherapy also shares Dr. Glasser's fundamental insight that healing is effected to the extent that an individual is led to accept reality and is enabled to fulfill his basic needs within the real world. For Christotherapy, however, it is above all in Christ that the real is encountered and the basic way is revealed in which an individual can best fulfill his needs within the real world.

The fundamental inspiration and key source of many of the central emphases and principles of Christotherapy is the existential psychotherapy of Dr. Thomas Hora, the distinguished New York psychiatrist. Christotherapy shares to an extent Dr. Hora's foundational insight that pathology, sickness, and disorder are a manifestation and consequence of a person's failure to be in harmony with God or Existence, and that the complete healing of the individual requires an enlightened, harmonious "At-One-Ment" with the Love-Intelligence that is God. Christotherapy supports Hora's view that there is an intrinsic connection between the realization within oneself of authentic religious values and the achievement of psychic, emotional, and somatic wholeness. Holiness and wholeness are inseparably related in the psycho-religious perspective of Christotherapy and of the existential psychotherapy of Hora.

In the present chapter I wish to engage in a brief "dialectic of therapies" by comparing and contrasting Christotherapy with the therapies of Frankl, Hora, and Glasser. Since Hora and Glasser have exercised a greater influence in my development of Christotherapy than has Dr. Frankl, I shall devote more attention to the comparison and contrast of Christotherapy with the therapies of Hora and Glasser than with Frankl's.

Logotherapy and Christotherapy

Viktor Frankl was gifted with a far-reaching insight when he grasped that the search for, and discovery of, meaning and value is crucial for the healing of many of the ills of modern man.[1] Frankl, as a psychiatrist and, more importantly, as a most humane and sensitive individual, clearly understood, particularly in terms of the crucible of his concentration-camp experiences, that one's only hope in the face of the apparent surd of suffering is to find a value and a meaning that make life worth living. Christotherapy is similar to Frankl's logotherapy in stressing that healing can come through the discovery—the "active reception"—of authentic meaning and value. Unlike logotherapy, however, Christotherapy specifies the exact source of ultimate meaning and value, Christ, the Word or Logos or Meaning itself made flesh. Christotherapy affirms the power of the Christ-meaning "actively received" to heal us in all the dimensions of our being—spiritual, psychic, emotional, and somatic. Christotherapy is fraternally related to Frankl's logotherapy in its basic emphasis on the healing power of meaning. But it differs in insisting that meaning itself has been made flesh in Christ and that the light of Christ is able to heal all those who are open to its beneficent presence.

Dr. Thomas Hora's Existential Psychotherapy

Fundamental to Dr. Hora's approach is his belief that Transcendental Reality, or God, is Love-Intelligence and that the human person is the image and likeness of God. For man to exist authentically is to be a translucent medium through which the light of God shines. Man in Hora's understanding participates in existence but is not its cause. For us to ignore the grounding reality of our existence and to fancy ourselves instead as the "makers" or "masters" of our existence is to be in conflict with the fundamental order of things. This can only mean disharmony, disorder, and even disease in one's life, brought about by a wrong relationship with the Ontological Ground of existence. For Hora *the* tragic element in the human condition is rooted in a cognitive deficiency which inclines us to seek to confirm ourselves as primary reality. Because of our striving for the confirmation of self as primary reality, we suffer mentally, emotionally, physically, and in our destiny. In other words, it is basically ignorance of true meaning and value, and of the authentic way to exist-in-the-world, which lies at the root of our futile, idolatrous attempts at radical confirmation of ourselves as primary reality.

Just as for Hora it is ignorance of the way to live authentically in the world which is at the root of our problems, so naturally enough for him it is enlightenment, or the understanding of that which truly is, that heals us. Enlightenment, however, is not some sterile, abstract intellectual event but a "loving mode of cognition" and it takes place only within a climate of love. Ignorance is not mere ignorance of such "neutral facts" as the periodic table in chemistry or the exact texture of moon dust, etc., but rather, the ignorance—at times an ignoring—of the deepest human and religious values and life-meanings. And enlightenment is not the grasp of "indifferent truths," but, at its highest levels is participation in the light of Love-Intelligence. In Hora's view, love and understanding are one in the enlightened human consciousness as Love and Intelligence are one in God.

Hora sees the search for wholeness and holiness as the loving quest for the truth that sets the human person free (John 8:32). For Hora, truth liberates, understanding transforms, and love heals. Hora sees men and women as reaching the highest level of healing and enlightenment when they transcend all dualisms and enter into the nondual realm of Love-Intelligence. In this understanding of the nature of self-transcendence love is viewed as a mode of cognition and the human person is revealed as an instrument, a medium, an image, a likeness of Love-Intelligence. For Hora the moment when God becomes real to us is when human consciousness in its highest level of self-transcendence becomes conscious of Love as that Intelligence which forever reveals itself as Understanding. It was such a moment Job was referring to when he exclaimed: "I have known Thee by the hearing of the ears, but now mine eye seeth Thee" (Job 42:5, KJV).

In the light of Hora's view that ignorance of the authentic mode of being-in-the-world is the source of human miseries

and disharmonies, the process of healing becomes for him a
matter of dispelling the darkness of illusion and opening
oneself, or better, allowing oneself to be opened, to Love-
Intelligence as the background without which the foreground of human beings and their world could not be. We
must allow our minds to be washed of all false mental
assumptions, inauthentic mind-sets, and conceptual, intellectualist schemes regarding the nature of the self, reality,
and what it means to exist-in-the-world. We must be
reverential, open, wakefully receptive and attentive to what
truly is and to the Love-Intelligence that is the ground of
being and the source of all light.

HORA'S EXISTENTIAL PSYCHOTHERAPY AND

CHRISTOTHERAPY

Hora emphasizes that ignorance of authentic meaning
and value is the source of many of our lamentable sufferings, diseases, and disharmonies, and that a stress on the
gravity of our cognitive deficiencies is important. The
Christotherapeutic viewpoint grounds all man's disharmonies, including existential ignorance, in the original and
personal sinfulness of mankind. The presence of existential
ignorance in an individual does not necessarily imply that
this condition is the result of one's own personal sin. It may
simply be the result of one's participation as a member in
the human family. For this reason a priest, minister, or
psychiatrist who discerns profound existential ignorance in
an individual may judge it to be therapeutically necessary
not even to broach the problem of sin in certain situations,
but rather, simply to create a climate of love in which gifts
of enlightenment may be received. Sin is, nonetheless, a
primal fact of human existence and it is a mistake to ignore
the fact of sin or to reduce sin to a form of inculpable

ignorance, thus eliminating the reality of free choice and its consequences. I am not implying that Hora denies the reality of sin or of free will, but in general he prefers not to speak in these terms, terms which I consider important elements in the total existential picture of the human person.

For many today the teaching on original sin is a "hard saying"; even Christians often tend either to deny any meaning to original sin or to view it as a necessary moment in man's evolution as he moves toward higher levels of self-actualization. From this perspective, sickness, ignorance, suffering, and death as we experience them are inevitable side effects on the path that leads to the evolutionary Omega Point. In my understanding of Christian teaching, original sin is a tragic, unnecessary, but all too real fact about the course of human development. Sickness, suffering, and death *as we experience* them are the results of sin and need not have been. As Paul in Romans points out, nature itself is cursed because of sin and is now deformed, impotent, and decadent (Romans 8:19-24), but is awaiting the total salvation and glorification of man in which it will share. I maintain that one must not gloss over the facts of original and individual sinfulness. In the light of Christ's redemptive suffering, dying, and rising, we can speak of the original sin as a "happy fault"; but such poetic license can never be used to deny or overlook the tragic dimension of the fall and the effects which flowed from it.

Hora further emphasizes the unity of love and understanding in the consciousness of the enlightened individual. Hora is an existentially oriented psychiatrist deeply influenced by Zen—he was initially a strict Freudian analyst; he sees dualism in all forms as an obstacle to healing. Because of this he stresses a holistic or unitary approach as the proper mode of perceiving reality. Hora indicates that

to understand truly means to "stand under," or to assume a
loving, reverential, receptive stance regarding the source of
enlightenment. It is only the humble, open, loving consciousness that is able to understand the mysteries of being
and of life and to be made full of light. Knowledge and love
in this instance are one, the dualism of intellect and will is
transcended and the individual dwells in harmony with
existence. Hora illustrates this transcendence of dualism by
the scriptural phenomenon of love and its sexual expression:

In biblical language, to know a woman means to have loved her in
the sexual act. This refers to a mode of knowing which is
synonymous with loving union, and, conversely, to a mode of
loving which is synonymous with and leads to knowing. To know
is to love, to love is to know. Knowledge which is love resolves
the subject-object split into union.[2]

In the enlightened consciousness, understanding and
love interpenetrate. Hora here echoes an insight which
many of the great philosophers and sages have shared. The
Socratic equation of virtue and knowledge was perhaps
ultimately grounded in the insight that true wisdom and
true virtue are inseparable and dwell together in the enlightened consciousness of the truly wise person, the
philosopher who is in love with the good, the true, and the
beautiful. Augustine writes: "Give me a lover and he will
catch my meaning." Augustine suggests that there is a
knowledge born of love which only the lover has and which
leads to an ever deeper knowledge and love. Shakespeare
writes that "love knows reasons that reason never fathoms"
and Pascal in a similar vein speaks of "the heart with its
reasons which reason does not understand." Pascal here
affirms a higher level of consciousness—the human heart
touched by God—where a certain knowledge is the fruit of
love and dwells within love. Finally, John Henry Cardinal

Newman found it necessary to distinguish between "notional assent" and "real assent." Notional assent to God's existence is a purely rational acceptance of the truth that God exists. Real assent to God's existence involves the total person in dynamic commitment to God with the whole heart as well as the mind. Hora, then, stands in a firm tradition in his emphasis on the unity of knowledge and love in the enlightened consciousness. And the previous chapter brought forth scriptural writings exemplifying the interpenetration of love and knowledge which is at the very heart of the healing-through-enlightenment process.

Finally, just as Hora stresses the need to overcome all forms of dualism and to enter into the nondual realm of Love-Intelligence, so he emphasizes the significance of Jesus Christ and accords to him a most sublime role as a manifester of the divine and as a revealer to man of the authentic way to exist in the world. Hora once remarked to me that it was through the prism of Zen that he first beheld Christianity in its pure form; but he at once added that the splendor of Christ is to him like the light of high noon in comparison with the radiance of other prophets, avatars, and holy men, which is like the light of dawn. Hora does not, however, speak or write about Christ's divine sonship in the same fashion as do the great christological councils and the major Christian denominations. Nor does he view man as being called to participate in the life of God as Triune, if I understand him correctly. In my view, however, it is vital in the full context of healing through enlightenment to stress the unique divinity of Christ—truly God and truly man—and the reality of our calling, not merely to be an image and likeness of God as Love-Intelligence, but to share in the very trinitarian life of God as children of the Father, brothers and sisters of the Son, and possessors of the Spirit.

Dr. William Glasser's Reality Therapy and Christotherapy

William Glassser practices a form of therapy which he has named reality therapy. In his book of the same title, *Reality Therapy*, Glasser presents his theory.[3] He calls his approach "reality therapy" because its purpose is to help patients deal successfully with the tangible and intangible aspects of the real world. Glasser's fundamental insight is that healing is effected to the extent that the patient comes to accept the real world and becomes able to fulfill his basic needs within the real world. Glasser holds that all patients share the common characteristic of denying the reality of the world around them. To the extent that they learn to fulfill their basic needs in the world as it actually is, they will have no inclination to deny it.

CHRIST, THE ULTIMATE REAL

Christotherapy shares with reality therapy the belief that operative in all the mentally ill—this is only one segment of the concern of Christotherapy—is a certain denial of true reality. Christotherapy, however, very often roots this denial in an existential ignorance, perhaps culpable and perhaps not, of true meaning and value, of the authentic way to exist-in-the-world. More importantly, Christotherapy stresses that reality as it really is, is grounded in and pervaded by Love-Intelligence, that Love-Intelligence has become incarnate in Jesus Christ, and that to be ignorant of the mystery of Love-Intelligence and of Jesus Christ is to be ignorant of the most important aspects of reality. Thus, just as Christotherapy goes beyond logotherapy in stressing that Love-Intelligence is the ground of being and that Logos itself is made flesh in Jesus Christ, so Christotherapy adds a further religious dimension to reality therapy and stresses that healing in coming to grips with reality involves, above all, encounter with the *Ultimate Real:* Love-Intelligence and its epiphany in Jesus Christ.

Glasser further indicates that for an individual to fulfill his basic needs, involvement with other people is necessary. At the very minimum we must each have one person whom we care about and who cares about us. Glasser does not insist that the essential person be in as close a relationship to us as a mother to a child or a teacher to his student, but it is necessary that no matter how distant the essential person is, we must have a strong feeling of this person's existence and he or she of ours. Another necessary characteristic for that essential person is to be in touch with reality and capable of fulfilling his or her own needs within the world.

Christotherapy shares Glasser's stress on the need for communion with an "essential person" if the individual is to come into accord with reality as it is and fulfill personal needs. Christotherapy—and this confirms the view of reality therapy even more—stresses that in the ordinary purpose of providence it is only through the encounter of loving, beneficent, benevolent persons that the reality of God's love for us becomes existentially mediated or "really real." John writes that "a man who does not love the brother that he can see / cannot love God whom he has never seen" (1 John 4:20). One might alter this affirmation somewhat and ask: "How is it possible for us if we have never experienced any love on the part of our brothers or sisters whom we see to have any 'real knowledge' of the love of the God whom we have never seen?" Christotherapy, in light of what has just been said, places great emphasis on the need for essential persons or, in the specific language of Christotherapy, of healed and enlightened persons, if basic human needs are to be fulfilled and, above all, if the reality of God's love—the basic need and desire of the human heart—is to be effectively mediated and communicated.

I must add that only those individuals in whom God's healing and enlightening grace and the gift of his love abide can love others in a lasting, full, and complete fashion. Because of my understanding of Christian teaching on the original and personal sinfulness of man, I do not believe that it is in fact existentially possible to remain constantly and fully and selflessly committed to another without the aid of Christ's grace and the indwelling of the gift of God's love. I am not implying that only explicit Christian believers can love in this total and permanent fashion. Anyone in whom the gift of God's love dwells, regardless of whether or not the individual is explicitly aware of the inner source and power of his love, is capable of being an essential person and a loving, beneficent presence in the world.

FULFILLMENT OF BASIC NEEDS

Glasser, after discussing the key role of the essential person, indicates that all persons have the same basic physiological and psychological needs. Psychiatry, then, in Glasser's view "must be concerned with two basic psychological needs; the need to love and be loved and the need to feel that we are worthwhile to ourselves and to others."[4]

Glasser emphasizes that the quest for fulfillment in the need to love and be loved is a constant throughout life. It is not enough simply to be loved by a mother or friend or spouse; it is essential also to love. Failure to fulfill in a lasting fashion the desire either to love or to be loved leads from a mild form of discomfort through severe anxiety and depression to a complete flight from reality as it is.

Christotherapy shares with reality therapy the belief that

the fulfillment of the need to love and be loved on the interhuman level is crucial for human development. But Christotherapy sees the deepest need and desire of the human heart as the need to love and be loved by God. If the gift of God's love is not present in the human heart, a person is of necessity in a state of alienation, restlessness, and unfulfillment. Although Christotherapy concurs with reality therapy on the need for loving communion with a fellow human being if basic love needs are to be fulfilled, it stresses that once Christ is mediated to an individual through another loving Christ-filled individual, then Christ can become an essential person in one's life. Christ is indeed a "tremendous lover," and love of him and loving belief in his love can sustain one in what otherwise are most loveless situations and bring about in a person ever-deepening healing. Paul expresses the power with which the love of Christ can grip and fill us when he writes: "The life I now live in this body I live in faith: faith in the Son of God who loved me and sacrificed himself for my sake" (Galatians 2:20).

ACTING RESPONSIBLY

Glasser also holds that the second basic human need is the need to feel that we are worthwhile to ourselves and to others. In his view, maintaining a satisfactory standard of behavior is a fundamental part of being worthwhile. For Glasser, then, values, morals, standards, right and wrong, are necessary factors in fulfilling the need to feel worthwhile. If we fail to live up to our moral standards we will suffer just as intensely as when we fail to love or be loved.

"Responsibility," then, is a key concept in reality therapy. To act responsibly is to fulfill one's needs without depriving others of the ability to fulfill their needs. Glasser offers the following example of responsible action:

A responsible person can give and receive love. If a girl, for example, falls in love with a responsible man, we would expect him either to return her love or to let her know in a considerate way that he appreciates her affection but that he does not share her feelings. If he takes advantage of her love to gain some material or sexual end, we would not consider him responsible.[5]

In Glasser's view the teaching of responsibility is our most important task and the central concern of reality therapy. Glasser stresses that the parent or counselor who is trying to bring the child or adult to act responsibly and so to fulfill basic needs and to feel worthwhile, must be loving and open but must never condone irresponsible activity. Finally, Glasser indicates that the therapist must also be one who acts responsibly if he or she is to be effective as a therapist.

Christotherapy and reality therapy believe that fulfillment of the basic need to feel worthwhile to ourselves and to others is necessary if we are to be healed and live in accord with reality as it really is. Both therapies stress responsible activity as an absolute prerequisite for fulfilling the need to feel worthwhile. Feeling worthwhile is authentic only if it flows from being worthwhile and from fidelity to the natural human drive to be responsible.

In Glasser's view human beings are, unlike animals, not driven by instinct to care for and teach "responsibility" to their young. Animals instinctively care for their young and teach them the art of healthy living and of survival. Human beings, however, in place of instinct have developed the mental resources to teach responsibility to their children. Christotherapy emphasizes that we possess a natural spiritual drive to be responsible and chooses with Hora to view responsibility within the perspective of Existence.[6] From this point of view responsibility essentially involves being responsible to the demands of Existence or God. "Response-ability" is an ability given by God to a person whereby one is able to respond to authentic value and most fundamentally to *the* Value: God. From this perspective responsibility is not a duty or burden but a gift, a privilege, a capacity for growth toward enlightenment. Responsibility enhances life, liberates us, and enables us to enjoy life in its harmonious unfolding and to be at one with Existence. It is through responsible action that we actively receive inner fulfillment. Bernard Lonergan lends support to this approach to responsibility when he stresses that to achieve authenticity and self-fulfillment it is necessary for an individual to obey the inner exigencies of the human spirit. Lonergan indicates that the imperative "Be Responsible!" is the culminating existential imperative in the series of what he terms the four transcendental precepts: Be Attentive! Be Intelligent! Be Reasonable! Be Responsible! Self-fulfillment, in Lonergan's terms, involves constant fidelity to these imperatives of the spirit. Failure to obey these dynamic spiritual exigencies puts us in a state of war with ourselves and precludes the possibility of the fulfillment of what Glasser terms the basic human need to be and feel worthwhile to oneself and to others.

Christotherapy and reality therapy both affirm that acting responsibly always involves acting in such a way that the needs of others to love and be loved and feel worthwhile to themselves and others are never interfered with. The law of love—of enemies as well as friends—is the fundamental moral principle of Christianity, and Glasser's rule is simply one specific application of the Christian principle of love. Finally, Christotherapy shares with reality therapy the premise that the therapist, to be effective, must be capable of fulfilling his basic needs within reality as it really is.

ATTITUDINAL VERSUS BEHAVIORAL CHANGE

Christotherapy and reality therapy differ somewhat in their respective emphases on behavioral and attitudinal change. Glasser writes: "In Reality Therapy we are much more concerned with behavior than with attitudes."[7] It is his view that changing behavior can lead quickly to a change in attitude and that waiting for attitude changes during therapy can stall the therapeutic process. Enlightenment, however, is the key moment in Christotherapy and it involves in its central form a conversion of mind and heart. Attitudinal rather than behavioral change is the core stress of Christotherapy because, as Jesus taught, it is from the heart that "come evil intentions: murder, adultery, fornication, theft, perjury, slander" (Matthew 15:19). Christotherapy believes, as does reality therapy, that irresponsible conduct should not be approved by the therapist. Christotherapy also urges the cessation of bad conduct and the practice of good deeds; but its basic aim is to bring the irresponsible or existentially ignorant individual to an understanding of the meaning of his inauthentic mode of being-in-the-world and hence to effect a change in conduct. Christotherapy acknowledges that a change in conduct may provide the occasion for an enlightenment or attitudinal change to occur; but only an inward enlightenment brings about true healing.

RELATIONSHIP BETWEEN "MENTAL-ILLNESS," IRRESPONSIBILITY, AND EXISTENTIAL IGNORANCE

Reality therapy rejects the concept of "mental illness" and speaks instead of irresponsibility. Glasser states that such terms as "neurotic," "psychotic," "schizophrenic," etc., should simply be considered as labels for describing various forms of irresponsible behavior. Glasser asks his readers to try to substitute *responsible* for *mental health* and *irresponsible* for *mentally ill*. In Glasser's perspective it is not helpful to give "mentally ill" persons the idea that their sickness is analogous to physical illness and that they therefore have no more responsibility in their condition than do cancer patients in the face of their illness. Glasser holds that all patients, no matter what psychiatric complaint they are suffering from, have in common that they are unable to fulfill their basic needs in a realistic fashion and hence resort to irresponsible, unrealistic modes of behavior in a futile effort at fulfillment. Glasser stresses that it is the task of the therapist to help the patients help themselves fulfill their needs *responsibly* and in this way to be healed. Christotherapy, like reality therapy, prefers to drop the term "mental illness" and to speak, rather, of the patient as existing in a state of existential ignorance and of being in need of healing through enlightenment as it occurs within a climate of love. Christotherapy shares to a large extent Dr. Hora's view that one is "ill" in existential psychiatric terms when one's existence is misdirected and fragmented. We are healed, however, to the extent that we allow our minds to be washed of their misdirected concerns or existential ignorance and awakened to the creative, harmonious, loving mode of being-in-the-world.

THE PRIMARY ROLE OF THE PRESENT IN THE HEALING PROCESS

Glasser stresses most forcefully that it is the *present* state of the individual patient and not the *past* that should be the focal concern in the therapeutic process. Glasser does not go into the past of his patients, their traumas, family relationships, etc., but rather, tries to bring the individual patient to fulfill his or her needs by acting responsibly in the present. Here, of course, Glasser breaks completely with the classical Freudian-based psychoanalytic approaches. Christotherapy, like reality therapy, also focuses primarily on the present state of the individual. Christotherapy says, with Paul: "Now is the favourable time; this is the day of salvation" (2 Corinthians 6:2). The principal effort of the Christotherapist, operating as an instrument of

Christ, is to bring the patient to an understanding of present misdirected modes of being-in-the-world and to indicate the authentic way to be, live, and act in the present. It is true that in the healing-through-enlightenment process the past will be illuminated; but in the view of Hora and Christotherapy, this is only a by-product and of secondary importance. Christotherapy follows Hora and agrees with Glasser that the *central stress* in therapy should be put on the present rather than the past.

PRACTICE OF REALITY THERAPY AND CHRISTOTHERAPY

Glasser affirms that the practice of reality therapy is not limited to professionals. The difference between reality therapy as professionally practiced and as applied in common guidance is a difference in intensity, not in kind. As Glasser indicates:

Anyone using the principles of Reality Therapy who attempts to help a person help himself toward more responsible behavior does nothing basically different from the psychiatrist or for that matter different from parents who try to the best of their ability to raise a child to be a responsible citizen.[8]

Christotherapy is like reality therapy to the extent that its "practice" by professionals or nonprofessionals is not a difference in kind. Christotherapy is also like reality therapy in that its principles can be technically developed and professionally applied. Christotherapy is *in principle* open to specific application in psychiatry, psychological counseling, pastoral guidance, etc. But I must add that Christotherapy can only be proposed and worked out within a specifically theological context, because this therapy in its central thrust is inspired by reflections on Scripture as mediated through the insights of contemporary existential psychotherapy.

Christ: The Unique Physician

In concluding I must stress that Christotherapy is unique in reference to most other well-known contemporary therapies in its emphasis on the role of Christ in the healing-through-enlightenment process. More specifically, the uniqueness of Christotherapy is its view that there is only one ultimate therapist—all others cooperate as his instruments. The one ultimate therapist is Jesus Christ, who is the way, the truth, and the life; the goal of the therapy is for those undergoing it to be transformed into the therapist so that in the end, as Augustine expresses it: "There will be one Christ loving himself."

NOTES

1. Viktor Frankl, *Man's Search for Meaning* (New York: Pocket Books, 1972).

2. Thomas Hora, "Epistemological Aspects of Existence and Psychotherapy," pp. 169–170.

3. William Glasser, *Reality Therapy* (New York: Harper & Row, 1965).

4. *Ibid.*, p. 9.

5. *Ibid.*, p. 13.

6. Thomas Hora, *In Quest of Wholeness*, ed. Jan Linthorst (Garden Grove, Calif.: Christian Counseling Service, Inc., 1972), pp. 63–72.

7. Glasser, *Reality Therapy*, p. 27.

8. *Ibid.*, p. 20.

III

Self, Christ-Self, and Self-Image

WHAT IS THE SELF? What is the meaning and role of self-image? These are significant existential questions. The famous precept of Socrates was: "Know thyself." Augstine's great prayer was: "Lord, grant that I may know myself and that I may know thee." A central concern of contemporary philosophy and theology is: What is the true, the real self? Many contemporary psychotherapies make growth in authentic self-knowledge and the development of a proper self-image pivotal in the process of psychic healing and human maturation. This chapter is concerned specifically with the question of the self. It begins with a discussion of the nature of the self and the Christ-self and, in light of those, analyses the meaning and function of self-image and the possibility of transformation in self-image.

Definitions of human nature and of the human self, or the individual, abound. Aristotle defined man as a rational animal. Plato, in some interpretations, defined man as a spirit imprisoned in matter. For Atomists like Democritus, the finest, smoothest, and most agile atoms constituted the human mind. In more recent times Karl Marx focused on man as an economic animal. In Sigmund Freud's conception man was largely a creature of desire and sexual orientation. Both Marx and Freud denied in the sharpest terms the spirituality of man. On the contemporary scene Jean-Paul Sartre affirms that man is a being condemned to be free and subject to internal contradiction at the core of his being. B. F. Skinner, in radical opposition to Sartre, loudly proclaims that human freedom is an illusion. For Skinner, in the final analysis, the human being is just as much subject to deterministic forces as are Pavlov's dogs. The definitions of man go on and on. . . .

The many blatant contradictions among the definitions of man suggest that not all of them can be correct. This causes concern because one's spontaneous or reflective understanding of what it is to be a human being has radical implications for the type of self-image he will develop, the type of life he will live, and the type of future he will have. Self-understanding and self-imaging are multileveled, highly complex processes, and for most individuals tend to be spontaneous and intuitive rather than deliberate and reflective. Yet the conscious quest for growth in understanding the nature of the self and the development of a more adequate self-image often involve the occurrence of enlightening insights within a climate of loving attentiveness and existential reflection.

Individuals follow many paths in their search for deeper, more authentic knowledge of the self. The present work affirms, however, that the truest path, the most radical and foundational explanation of the nature of the self, is located in the Hebrew and New Testament revelations culminating in Christ.

Scriptural revelation and the reflections of Christian tradition on the nature of man and of the human self are rich and multidimensional. In the present context two key revelations about the self are considered. First, there is

God's gift to man of selfhood itself, i.e., the gift of existence as human beings. Second, there is God's gift to those he has created of adoption as his own children in Christ. God first gives selfhood to man so that he may then invite man to enter into loving communion with himself. Genesis recounts God's gift to man of basic selfhood in the words: "God created man in the image of himself, / in the image of God he created him" (Genesis 1:27). The epistle to the Ephesians reveals God's second great gift to man in its opening chapter: "Blessed be God the Father of our Lord Jesus Christ. . . . Before the world was made, he chose us in Christ . . . determining that we should become his adopted sons, through Jesus Christ" (Ephesians 1:3-5).

The Self and Its Key Characteristics

In considering God's first gift to man, the self, and God's second gift to man, the gift of adoption as children in Christ, it is necessary on occasion also to reflect on some negative factors. This is because to the self there is opposed the antiself and to the Christ-self there is opposed the anti-Christ-self. Healing comes through correct understanding of, and living in accordance with, the self and the Christ-self, and wounding and darkening come through misunderstanding the nature of the self and the Christ-self and the doomed attempt to "live," instead, according to the specious requirements of the antiself and the anti-Christ-self. Both the negative and positive elements are necessary as a background for the consideration of the role of self-image in the healing-through-enlightenment process.

Genesis is referring to the gift of selfhood itself when it relates that God created man in his own image and likeness. The revelation of the meaning of man's basic or natural selfhood constantly deepens throughout the Hebrew Testament period and reaches its permanent apex in Christ. In the Church the Holy Spirit continuously leads the People of God to a richer understanding of the nature of selfhood revealed in Christ. Among the key characteristics of the self in the Christian perspective are: the self is at once social and individual; it is incarnate spirit; it is servant and master (created and creative); it is intelligent and free; it is naturally good, but capable of evil.

The Self as Social

The first reference to man in the Old Testament is in the plural. "God said, 'Let us make man in our own image, in the likeness of ourselves' " (Genesis 1:26). The social, communitarian dimension of man is stressed throughout the Hebrew Testament period. The man is complemented by the woman and individuals are viewed largely in terms of their membership in the tribe and nation. Radically isolated individuality is alien to the Hebrew Testament view of man. It is not good for man to be alone.

In the New Testament period there is also great stress on the social dimension of basic human selfhood. Christ, in Matthew's sermon, teaches his followers to pray: "Our Father in heaven" (Matthew 6:9). Paul tells the Corinthians: "Now you together are Christ's body" (1 Corinthians 12:27). In Matthew God's ultimate judgment of man is predicated on how man has dealt with his fellow man with whom Jesus identifies himself (Matthew 25:31-46). The author of Ephesians writes that "he [God] chose *us* in Christ" (Ephesians 1:4). The book of Revelation portrays the heavenly Jerusalem as filled with a great crowd singing, "Alleluia! Victory and glory and power to our God" (Revelation 19:1). The New, like the Hebrew, Testament constantly emphasizes the essentially social nature of man.

Human beings are seen as members of one another and by
their very nature ordered to one another. Anything like the
Hobbesian view of man as essentially "a wolf to man" is
absent. In the light of the New Testament perspective any
view of man as being essentially or naturally antisocial
belongs to the realm of the antiself and the anti-Christ-self.
(By antiself and by anti-Christ-self is meant any understanding of man or choice or action of man which is
opposed to the Christian understanding of selfhood and the
Christ-self.)

The Self as Individual

In the Hebrew and New Testament revelations there is
great stress on the social dimension of human selfhood, but
the unique value of the self in its individuality is also
proclaimed. The Hebrew Testament indicates that God
created human individuals, males and females, and that he
valued these individuals in themselves. Hebrew Testament
accounts are studded with the names of individuals whom
Yahweh loved, called by name, and chose to carry out his
will. To the prophet Jeremiah, Yahweh said: "Before I
formed you in the womb I knew you; before you came to
birth I consecrated you; I have appointed you as prophet to
the nations" (Jeremiah 1:5). And the book of Wisdom
teaches that there is an immortal aspect to the individual:
"The virtuous live for ever, / their recompense lies with the
Lord, / the Most High takes care of them" (Wisdom
5:15-16).

The value of selfhood in its individuality is proclaimed
above all in Christ. Jesus Christ in his own individuality is
of eternal significance and each man who perseveringly
believes in him, even though he undergoes physical death,
shall live forever. Jesus in his lifetime showed great affec-

tion and concern for individuals. Of the rich young man, Mark writes that Jesus "looked steadily at him and loved him" (Mark 10:21). The evangelist John describes himself as "the disciple Jesus loved" (John 13:23). John likewise portrays Jesus as the good shepherd who calls his sheep by name and who knows them just as the Father knows him (John 10:3, 14-15). Perhaps nowhere in the New Testament is Jesus' love for the individual more sharply etched than in the words of Paul, words which each one of us as individuals can appropriate for ourselves: "I live in faith: faith in the Son of God who loved me and who sacrificed himself for my sake" (Galatians 2:20). Finally, the book of Revelation clearly indicates the eternal value of the individual. "To those who prove victorious I will give the hidden manna and a white stone—a stone with a new name written on it, known only to the man who receives it" (Revelation 2:17). In Christ the gift of selfhood is clearly revealed as a pearl of great price, a treasure of everlasting value and significance.

Authentic self-understanding within the Christian perspective involves an appreciation and a cherishing of both the communal and the individual dimensions of human selfhood. Thus, the Christian is commanded to love his neighbor *as he loves himself*. Husbands are told to love their wives just as they love their own bodies (Ephesians 5:28). In the Christian scheme of things there is a good, holy, and necessary self-love, a joy in one's individuality as such, just as there is also the love of neighbor. There is a healing that comes to man through the existential understanding that fulfillment comes to man through the proper love of self and of the neighbor in Christ.

There is no room in the Christian perspective for a vision of man which deprecates individual selfhood. The conception of selfhood or individuality or the ego as something evil or imperfect or something to be completely transcended and abolished is a fundamental expression of the antiself.

There is such a phenomenon as egotism or an exaggerated individualism. But just because egotism exists, there is no justification for denouncing the ego itself as evil. Just because there is exaggerated individualism there is no justification for individuality itself to be called evil. Egotism and exaggerated individualism are in opposition to the nature of authentic selfhood and are thus forms of the antiself. It does no good to attempt to root out excessive individualism and egotism by seeking to destroy the ego or individuality. The latter type of endeavor, regardless of the good will which at times might inspire it, is rooted in a fundamental misconception of the nature of the self, and therefore cannot lead to authentic growth or healing through enlightenment.

The Self as Incarnate Spirit

Christian reflection on the truths of revelation discloses that man is incarnate spirit, a unity of the spiritual and the material. Man is capable of both intellectual and sense operations and this indicates that man is truly flesh as well as open in the depths of his being to the spiritual and the transcendent.

Authentic Christian understanding of the nature of the self involves the valuing of man in both his spiritual and his material dimensions. The Christian understanding of man opposes any view which deprecates the somatic dimension of man for the sake of exalting spirit or which denies the spirituality of man in the name of the excellence of matter. For the Christian the body is good and beautiful just as is the spirit. In fact, Christianity so values man in his bodily as well as in his spiritual dimensions that it preaches the resurrection of the body. Jesus has risen from the dead and exists forever in a glorified bodily state. Those who love the

Lord faithfully are called to share in the glorious resurrected state of Christ. There is then a healing that comes to the individual who understands that it is good, very good to be human, to be incarnate spirit, and it will eternally be so.

The Self as Servant and Master

The self is characterized as being at once servant and master (created and creative). Genesis portrays man as created by God, subject to God, called to be obedient to God:

Yahweh God took the man and settled him in the garden of Eden to cultivate and take care of it. Then Yahweh God gave the man this admonition, "You may eat indeed of all the trees in the garden. Nevertheless of the tree of the knowledge of good and evil you are not to eat, for on the day you eat of it you shall most surely die."

Genesis 2:15-17

Through his command to man Yahweh indicates that man is not a totally autonomous being, sole "captain of his fate and master of his soul" but, rather, a servant subject to his maker. God is the creator of man, and his command, far from being arbitrary or capricious, flows from his knowledge of what truly fulfills the heart of man. So, the psalmist writes: "The precepts of Yahweh are upright, / joy for the heart; / the commandment of Yahweh is clear, / light for the eyes" (Psalm 19:8).

Genesis also depicts man as one called to be creative and master in the world. "God said, . . . Let them be masters . . ." (Genesis 1:26). God tells his creature man to "be fruitful, multiply, fill the earth and conquer it" (Genesis 1:28). And the psalmist says of man:

You have made him little less than a god, you have crowned him
with glory and splendor, made him lord over the work of your
hands, set all things under his feet.

Psalm 8:5-6

Scripture portrays man as kingly and godlike in his domin-
ion over the earth and yet as totally dependent on God and
subject to him in all things. And man is only truly creative
and successful in his rule over the kingdom of the earth to
the extent that he is perfectly obedient to the Lord of
Heaven.

In his existential psychotherapeutic practice Thomas
Hora places very strong emphasis on the need for the
individual to be constantly responsive to the demands of
Existence or that Love-Intelligence that is God. Hora uses
differences which exist between Western and Eastern puppet theater to bring out man's radical dependence on God as
the ground of existence. In the West invisible puppeteers
control the puppets from behind the scenes and try to
create the illusion of maximum independence on the part of
the puppets. In the East, especially in Japan, the puppeteer
remains fully visible at all times and moves the puppets in
such a way that the audience is conscious at every moment
of the puppeteer's relationship to the puppets as their
animating source. In Japanese puppet theater, Hora notes,
the puppets "are manifold manifestations and expressions
of that power which animates them and which represents
the basis of their being."[1] The puppets and puppeteer are,
for Hora, symbolic expressions of man's contingency and
inseparable dependence on God. In Hora's view man's
whole existence is a call to respond to Existence, or God, by
manifesting him, by showing forth his light. And the more
complete man's response to Love-Intelligence is, the more
harmonious, healthy, liberating, and creative will be man's
presence in the world. Of course, the analogy of man as a
puppet falters, since man is endowed with intelligence and

freedom and above all responds to existence and manifests the light of Love-Intelligence through intelligent and free activity. Yet, in the Christian scheme of things man is in a radical sense even more dependent on God than are puppets on a puppeteer, for "it is in him that we live, and move, and exist" (Acts 17:28), and "it is God, for his own loving purpose, who puts both the will and the action" into man (Philippians 2:13). So total is man's dependence on God that Karl Rahner was able to write: "When man says No [i.e., sins] it is his own work; when he freely says Yes he must attribute this to God as God's gift."[2] Man's dependence on God is such that his own free choices are God's own gifts. *All is gift.* There is absolutely nothing which man possesses simply on his own. Paul can thus write: "What do you have that was not given to you? And if it was given, how can you boast as though it were not?" (1 Corinthians 4:7).

There is a great healing that comes to man through his understanding of his absolute dependence on God and the realization that "all is gift." A gift is a constant reminder of the giver and a wellspring of thanksgiving. The realization that all gifts, including the self and every good thought and desire and action that flow from the self, descend from the Father of light (James 1:17) inspires constant mindfulness of the graciousness of that Existence by which our being is posited.

The Self as Intelligent and Free

The Genesis texts already considered indicate man's primal endowment with the gifts of intelligence and freedom. The self is above all created in the image and likeness of God insofar as it is innately gifted with the unrestricted capacity to know, to choose, to love, and to act in freedom.

What is initially most significant in regard to man's intelligence and freedom is dynamic potentiality. Man is created with an unrestricted desire for knowledge and value but these dynamic potentialities must be gradually actualized. Man is called to receive the gift of knowledge and to respond to values as they reveal themselves. Man's initial experience is of a hunger for a knowledge of being not yet possessed and of a desire to respond to values not yet unveiled. Man is called to be attentive to the data of experience so that the gift of insight may be bestowed; he is summoned to be understanding and insightful in the hope that he may move toward knowledge and the real; he is called to be rational so that he may reach a judgment through which some reality may be affirmed; finally, he is called to be responsible, that is to respond to value in an authentic fashion, so that he may be ever more loving and become an originating source of the good and value for others. In a word, man is a being with a vocation to receive actively the gift of knowledge and to respond to true values as they manifest themselves within the horizon of his spirit.

Man is capable not only of discovering or uncovering meaning and value but also of constituting meaning and values. The worlds of culture and technology are human creations full of meaning and value. Man is creative as well as receptive in the realm of meaning and value, but his basic stance is one of receptivity. It is only because he is initially receptive and responsive, and to the extent that he is authentically receptive and responsive, that he becomes capable of creativity in the domains of meaning and value.

In the light of the essentially dynamically receptive character of man's knowing, a German philosopher has pointed out a relationship between *Denken* and *Danken*, between thinking and thanking. To think fruitfully is to be "gifted with insight," and since thinking is always a matter of the reception of a gift, thanking is the spontaneous fruit of all thinking. An existential understanding of the true nature of thinking heals man of his tendency to be rudely calculating and demanding rather than reverential and humble in his quest for truth. "I bless you, Father, Lord of heaven and of earth, for hiding these things from the learned and the clever and revealing them to mere children" (Matthew 11:25).

Just as a person's insights are a gift, so his authentic choices made in true freedom are also a gift. And here we are in the realm of mystery and paradox. God is the initiator, the prime operator and consummator in all of the individual's deciding and doing as well as in his knowing; but at the same time the human person is truly free. Thus, the Church of Christ at one and the same time teaches that the individual's free choices and the good works that he does are gifts of God, and yet that they are not gifts of God in such a fashion that they are not also free choices and good deeds of the individual.

The natural self is endowed with the gift of freedom and, although freedom is God's greatest natural gift to man, due to man's finite nature it involves the possibility of failure. In creating man God did not and could not constitute another God, but He could and did bring into being a creature capable of freely becoming that which he is called to be. Man's freedom, then, his ability to accept freely the gifts of self-realization and self-transcendence, is at once that quality which makes the natural self most godlike but which also opens it to the possibility of radical failure. Unlike the flower, which inevitably and by a certain natural necessity blossoms and blooms in the presence of sunlight, the natural self can either lovingly consent to the inner exigency to grow and the gracious summons of the kingdom of truth, being, and value, or it can fail to develop, fail to respond authentically and so lapse into nonbeing, into dark servitude to the antiself.

Man is that being whose freedom can be the source of life or the occasion for death. Scripture reveals the possibilities open to man when it puts the following words on Moses' lips: "I set before you life or death, blessing or curse" (Deuteronomy 30:19). Moses, of course, immediately adds, "Choose life" *(ibid.)* but he will not force man to become that which he is summoned to be, for this would be to strip created freedom of its signifcance.

Not only the Hebrew and New Testaments, but the whole of Christian tradition emphasizes strongly the central role and importance of choice and decision in the process of human growth and Christian maturation. Moses said to his people: "Choose!" Christ constantly invited those around him to take a stand in his regard: "Come!" (John 1:39). "He who is not with me is against me" (Matthew 12:30). "Look, I am standing at the door, knocking. If one of you hears me calling and opens the door, I will come in" (Revelation 3:20). This emphasis on decision is reiterated throughout the centuries in the Church and in the actions and writings of the holy ones of God. Ignatius of Loyola makes the "election," or decision, a very important element in Jesuit spirituality and it plays a key role in his *Spiritual Exercises.*

The central importance of decision is also brought out in contemporary psychotherapies. Dr. Harold Greenwald, in a work he entitles *Decision Therapy*, wrote that after working for some twenty years as a therapist he came to realize that "the only thing that happens in therapy, regardless of the methods or techniques used, is that the person you're working with is helped to make a *decision to change*, and then is helped to carry out the decision."[3] Greenwald found that by focusing on the role decision plays both in the development of psychological problems and in bringing about their resolution, he was able to be an instrument of healing in many areas, including addiction and various forms of compulsive or destructive behavior.

Christotherapy differs from Greenwald's decision therapy in that it situates decision within the context of the gift of enlightenment and, more specifically, of Christian enlightenment. Yet, Christotherapy shares with Greenwald the conviction that the capacity for decision is one of the endowments of the human self, and that the decisions and choices individuals make do play a critical role in determining the psychic health or illness of the individuals. Healing comes, then, through an existential understanding of the meaning and reality of freedom and its growth or decline, the life or death which flow from its proper use or abuse.

The Self as Good but Capable of Evil

The self is by its nature, in its basic dynamics and orientation, a drive for the meaningful, the true, the real, the worthwhile, the good, the beautiful, the divine. The precepts "Be attentive," "Be understanding," "Be reasonable," "Be responsible," "Be loving" are simply the thematic expression of the deepest exigencies of the natural self created in the image and likeness of God. The true self, then, is the self or natural self in its essential orientation; one is true to oneself to the extent that one obeys the sweet exigencies of the spirit.

It is therapeutically and religiously important to stress the essential goodness of the self in its natural dynamics because man is subject to a perennial temptation toward total self-depreciation and self-hatred; yielding to this deluded form of self-torture is the source of great and needless pain.

To affirm the essential goodness of the self is not to deny the reality of original and personal sin and the fact that the human person is subject to concupiscence and other effects of sin. Yet, despite the reality of sin, man's basic nature

remains good in its essential orientations toward the intel-
ligible, the true, the real, the worthwhile. Neither original
nor personal sin has blotted out or destroyed the image of
God in man. The Church has always insisted that sin has
not in such a way affected man that the self is altogether
stripped of its divine likeness and rendered totally incapable
of authentic intellectual and moral activities. Despite the
brutal fact of sin, in the words of the poet Hopkins, "there
lives the dearest freshness deep down things."[4]

The Confucian philosopher Mencius's stress on the
natural goodness of man involves an insight into the presence in man's essential self of a divine spark, and healing
can come through attending to the truth in the Chinese
sage's philosophy of man. Mencius considered human
nature to be constituted for the realization of goodness.
Heaven has endowed all men with a natural love for the
beauty of virtue and the worthwhile. As Mencius expressed
it: "Human nature tends to goodness just as water tends to
the low places. There is no man who does not tend to
goodness, just as there is no water that does not tend to low
places."[5] The doctrine of Mencius must be complemented
by the truths of revelation about the original and personal
sinfulness of man, the reality of concupiscence and subjec-
tion to death, and man's absolute need for Christ if he is to
be saved. Yet Mencius is correct in his vision of the
essential self as good. It is never authentic for an individual
to say that in the depths of his natural self he is utterly
worthless and full of rot and corruption. The self is created
in the image and likeness of God, and as long as life lasts
and the possibility for growth and self-transcendence is still
present, an individual can and should love and reverence
the spark of the divine that is in him and acknowledge and
cherish the "dearest freshness" at the fount of his selfhood.

The self is capable of failing to be authentic, to be
understanding, to be rational, to be responsible, to be

loving. To the extent that the self fails to become that which it is summoned to be there is a certain hollow, a privation, an absence of being in the midst of being which "appears." The name of this cipher or hollow in being is the antiself. The antiself is the false self. It is the shadow, the shell, the caricature of the true self. Disease, disharmony, ignorance, and sin are typical "features" of the antiself. When to the failure to obey the natural exigencies of the spirit there is added a rejection of the light of Christ, the anti-Christ-self appears. The anti-Christ-self is everything in man opposed to the Christ. Finally, if there is a definitive and lasting rejection of the exigencies of the self and of the Christ-self then the zero-self, the self of the "second death," the Hell-self is born only to die forever, since its birth is eternal death itself. In a book on light and healing it is necessary to mention the ultimate perversion, the Hell-self, since Christ often spoke of it in the most frightful terms. But this book is written for the living and not for the eternally dead, and for us there is hope. In fact, we are commanded to hope, and are called toward self-transcendence and transformation into the Christ-self and finally into the perfect self.

The Christ-Self

The apostle Paul in his epistle to the Romans writes:

We know that by turning everything to their good God cooperates with all those who love him, with all those that he has called according to his purpose. They are the ones he chose specially long ago and intended to become true images of his Son, so that his Son might be the eldest of many brothers.

Romans 8:28-29

The most significant revelation God has made to mankind about himself is the disclosure that he is Father, Son, and

Spirit. God unveiled for us the mystery of his "inner faces" by telling us what we are called to be in his Son, the Christ. The richest word God has spoken to us about ourselves is that we are called to be brothers and sisters of Christ, sharers in the divine nature and participants in the dynamic inner life of the trinitarian God. To this end the Father "sent his Son, born of a woman" to redeem us and "to enable us to be adopted as sons" (Galatians 4:5). Moreover, the Father has sent "the Spirit of his Son into our hearts: the Spirit that cries, 'Abba, Father'" (Galatians 4:6). God's love is poured forth into our hearts by the Spirit (Romans 5:5) and through the power of the Spirit, Christ's Spirit and our own through God's gift, we are enabled to call the Father "Abba."

The richest aspect of our transformation into the Christ-self is our ability to call the Father "Abba" just as Jesus did. The Aramaic word *abba* means "father," but as a diminutive form it is correctly translated "daddy." Children at the time of Jesus used the term to address their fathers affectionately. Jesus' use of the term "Abba" in reference to Yahweh often shocked certain Jews. Jesus' use of the term was a sign of his unique relationship with the Father. It is of the greatest healing significance that through the gift of Christ's Spirit we too are able to address the Father with the daringly intimate term "Abba." Through the incarnation, death, and resurrection of Christ we are offered the power to become children of the Father, brothers and sisters of the Son, and possessors of the Spirit of the Father and the Son. The richest form of healing comes then to the Christian who "dares" to call the Father "Abba" and who makes the Father the vital center of his consciousness, just as the Father was and forever is the center of the consciousness of Jesus the Christ. There is no room in authentic Christian consciousness for any view which would urge the Christian to drop the word "God" from his vocabulary or to cease to call the Father "Abba." Today, more than ever, the Christian should joyously "dare" to call God "Father" and to trust in him as the infant trusts the human father who dandles him or her in his arms.

The full reality of man's participation in the Christ-self is a mystery which exceeds human comprehension. Among the varied dimensions of transformation into the Christ-self are the sacramental, the moral, the ascetical, the ontological, the illuminative, and the mystical. Each of these modes of participation in the Christ-self is rich in meaning and should be the subject of constantly deepening meditation and healing contemplation.

Sacramental Participation

The role of the sacraments in Christian living will be dealt with later at some length. Here a few comments will suffice. Through the sacraments, which are the visible signs of Christ's invisible grace, we are transformed into the likeness of Christ in diverse ways. In baptism we are buried with Christ and also raised up with him to a newness of life. And, in the Eucharist, the sacrament par excellence, we eat the flesh of Christ and drink his blood and become one with him, so metamorphosed into him that he is more intimate to us than we are to ourselves. St. John Chrysotom expresses well the intensity and depth of union with Christ and transformation into Christ realized in the Eucharist when he puts these words on the lips of the Saviour:

I left my Father and came to thee, to thee who didst hate me, who didst flee me, who didst not even wish to hear my name, I followed thee, I ran after thee, I caught hold of thee, and embraced thee. "Eat me" I said and "Drink me." I want nothing to come between us. I wish the two to become one.[6]

Transformation into the Christ-self through the sacraments
and other means does not imply the obliteration of the
individual self. All things were created in Christ in their
unique individuality and he holds all things together in a
unity (Colossians 1:15-18). To be in Christ and transformed
into the Christ-self is to become most fully oneself. For
God wills "all perfection to be found in him [Christ] and all
things to be reconciled through him and for him" (Colossians 1:19-20).

Moral and Ascetical Participation

Christ is not only the Logos or Word made flesh, he is
also incarnate value. To participate in the Christ-self is to
be morally converted, to be ruled not by desire and fear, by
mere personal satisfaction, but by the authentic values revealed in Christ. The follower of Christ is to consider himself dead to sin but alive to true value in Christ. Moral
transformation into the Christ-self is highly ascetical and
involves a dying to all that is inauthentic and an uncompromising commitment to the truly good and worthwhile as
unveiled in the event of Jesus.

Ontological Participation

The ontological participation can be called a "real" participation in the Christ-self. Christ is our very life in a real
and not merely figurative sense (John 14:6; 10:10). Christ
himself through his Spirit dwells within those who love
him as a new principle of life and activity. And this indwelling and presence is as real as the being of our natural
selves. "Anyone who is joined to the Lord is one spirit with
him" (1 Corinthians 6:17). Christ is our resurrection and life

and the vine in which we as living branches thrive and have our new being and our new self. As Paul writes: "He [Christ] is your life" (Colossians 3:4). Even though this life is at present "hidden . . . in God" (Colossians 3:3), it is so real and so true that when Christ appears in glory he will transfigure our very bodies "into copies of his glorious body" (Philippians 3:21). The human person's participation in the Christ-self penetrates to the depths of his being and involves the ultimate transfiguration of his bodily as well as his spiritual existence.

Illuminative Participation

As is the case with the forms of enlightenment, the various modes of participation in the Christ-self interpenetrate one another to an extent. Since the reality of the Christ-self is inexhaustible in its richness of meaning, it is useful to view it from diverse perspectives. Thus the illuminative aspect of participation in the Christ-self pertains to sharing in the being of Christ through religious knowledge and love. Paul was referring to this dimension of assimilation to Christ when he wrote: "The life I now live in this body I live in faith: faith in the Son of God who loved me and sacrificed himself for my sake" (Galatians 2:20). The author of Ephesians refers to this same type of participation in the Christ-self when he prays that Christ may dwell through faith in the hearts of believers (Ephesians 3:17). Again and again throughout the various epistles of Paul or of Pauline inspiration, the hope and prayer is expressed that the readers may grow in an interior wisdom and understanding of the unsearchable riches of Christ. It is revealed that the sublime calling of the believer is to put on Christ and to have the mind of Christ. Finally, by contemplating the glorious mystery of Christ we, in Paul's words, "with our unveiled faces reflecting like mirrors the brightness of the Lord, all grow brighter and brighter as we are turned into the image that we reflect" (2 Corinthians 3:18). Thus Paul proclaims the deepest meaning of the enlightenment process.

Mystical Participation

In terminology borrowed from Bernard Lonergan, the mystical is the being of the subject in Christ as opposed to the being of substance in Christ. When there is just the being of substance "it is being in love with God without awareness of being in love."[7] The being of the subject in Christ, however, is a matter of awareness:

In ways you all have experienced, in ways some have experienced more frequently or more intensely than others, in ways you still have to experience, and in ways none of us in this life will ever experience, the substance in Christ Jesus becomes the subject in Jesus Christ. For the love of God, being in love with God, can be as full and as dominant, as overwhelming and as lasting an experience as human love.[8]

Mystical participation in the Christ-self is a heightened conscious experience of the Spirit of Christ working his transforming work within the human spirit through the gift of love. William Johnston has written of this experience of transformation into the Christ-self:

It [mystical enlightenment] reaches its climax when one's ego is lost to be replaced by that of Christ: "I live, now not I, but Christ liveth in me"; when one's consciousness is lost to be replaced by that of Christ: "Let that mind be in you which was in Christ Jesus"; it reaches its climax in a Trinitarian experience. "Now this is eternal life that they may know Thee the One true God and Jesus Christ whom Thou has sent."[9]

The Perfect Christ-Self

Beyond the mystical Christ-self there is the perfect Christ-self. The perfect Christ-self is the holy, spotless, glorified self one is called eternally to be in the resurrected state or in the "beatific participation." "Beatific participation" expresses heaven or man's final state because this state is not so much a matter of looking at God as it is a matter of dynamic participation in the inner life of God as Triune.

The apostle Paul is referring to the realization of the perfect Christ-self when he writes in Corinthians that "the knowledge that I have now is imperfect; but then I shall know as fully as I am known" (1 Corinthians 13:12). And it is of the resurrected, ascended and glorified self that the author of Revelation is speaking when he writes: "To those who prove victorious I will give the hidden manna and a white stone—a stone with a new name written on it, known only to the man who receives it" (Revelation 2:17). About this text George MacDonald writes:

The giving of the White Stone with the new name is the com-
munication of what God thinks about the man to the man. . . .
The true name is one which expresses the character, the nature,
the meaning of the person who bears it. . . . Who can give a man
this, his own name? God alone. For no one but God sees what the
man is. . . . It is only when the man has become his name that
God gives him the stone with his name upon it, for then first can
he understand what his name signifies.[10]

The perfect Christ-self is the antithesis of the zero-self, the anti-Christ-self. It is up to each individual to choose what self he wishes to become, what final name he wishes eternally to bear. The Father and his Christ say: Choose life! And, to as many as freely receive him and open themselves to his transforming power and healing light, Christ gives "power to become children of God" (John 1:12) and to be transformed into his glorious image.

Self-Image and Transformation in Self-Image

The human person as he exists and lives on this globe of the earth is in the process of becoming. He exists somewhere between zero and infinity. Psychologists and philosophers speak of man's need for self-actualization, self-realization, self-transcendence. Holy Scripture indicates that man is called to strive toward wholeness and holiness, toward the perfection of maturity in Christ. Terms such as self-actualization can be employed properly within a Christian context because God does not work in man in such a way that man is not also a free cooperator in the process of growth. So Revelation speaks of the good works and labors of a person that follow him into glory, so that he shall be rewarded for his deeds (Revelation 2:23; 14:13; 22:12; cf. also James 2:14; 2:17). At the same time it is God in Christ who is alpha and omega, the initiator and completer of all the individual's thoughts and deeds. Without God's gracious summons man cannot take one step toward salvation, and in every stage of his self-transcendence God is the sustaining power and the primary operator. God is the transcendent one; in him, and through the power of his grace, man freely transcends toward the Omega Point and the realization of the perfect Christ-self.

In the God-initiated and God-consummated process of self-transcendence, self-image and transformation of self-image play an important role. Here it is important to distinguish between the individual's present self or the self he presently happens to be and the perfect Christ-self, the self that the person is called by God to freely, ultimately become. For there is a gap between what the person presently is and what he is called to become—and self-image and transformation in self-image are mediating factors between what is presently in the individual and what is yet to be.

Present Self

The present self means the total self or the human being as he or she is here and now in all his or her concreteness and individuality. Thus, the present self is the historically and culturally and religiously conditioned person each one of us is right now with all of our individuating qualities, histories, idiosyncrasies, and defects of whatever nature. The present self is who each one of us is here and now emotionally, physically, morally, religiously, etc. More cosmically, the present self is each one of us who, as a member of the community of mankind, has through the primal sin of Adam been originally deprived of God's free gift of participation in his own divine nature. But the present self is also each one of us who through the death and resurrection of the New Adam, Jesus Christ, is called to be a son or daughter through the Son in an inchoate fashion in this life and perfectly in the life to come.

Self-Image

There is an inevitable gap between the self I presently happen to be and the images I have of myself both as I am and as I hope to be. Dr. Maxwell Maltz, plastic surgeon and author of the popular work *Psycho-Cybernetics*,[11] observes that even after plastic surgery a certain number of his patients still cling to the self-image of themselves as physically ugly persons although surgery has corrected their deformities. Maltz concludes that for some of his patients it is just as important, if not more important, to help effect an internal change in self-image as it is to bring about a cosmetic improvement through plastic surgery. In Maltz's view the self-image plays a dynamic and at times dramatic role in human maturation, and he provides sufficient evidence to more than justify his emphasis on the importance of self-image.

What, then, is self-image? The self-image is, like the self, a complex reality. Cecil Osborne defines the self-image as "the conscious and unconscious feelings you have about yourself."[12] Maltz describes the self-image as

your own conception of the sort of person you are. It is a product of past experiences, successes and failures, humiliations, and triumphs, and the way other people react to you, especially in early childhood. From these factors, and from others . . . you build up a picture of yourself which you believe is true.[13]

These two popular definitions capture basic traits of the self-image. The self-image involves a conception of the self; feelings about the self; and elements of both a conscious and an unconscious nature. Man is at once a rational being who inquires, understands, conceptualizes, reflects, judges, decides, loves and acts, and an emotional, imaginative, symbol-using being who feels intensely. As Lonergan observes, "it is feeling that gives to the rational dimension of man's consciousness its mass, momentum, drive, power."[14] In fact, "without these feelings . . . [man's] knowing and deciding would be paper thin."[15] Feelings are as constitutive of the self-image as are concepts, though I do believe, with Dr. Albert Ellis, that the type of feelings we experience is in large measure the result of ideas we firmly hold about the self, life, what "ought to be," etc. In any case, it may generally be said that both concepts and feelings pertain to the self-image, and consequently a transformation in self-image will involve a change on both the conceptual and the feeling level.

Transformation of Self-Image

The issue of transformation of self-image is of critical importance because an individual tends to operate in accord with the image he has of himself, and his operations in turn tend to confirm him in his self-image and to mold the self in accord with the self-image. If an individual is convinced that he is a born failure he will often tend in his activities to live out and consequently bear out his convictions about the self. A certain self-fulfilling prophecy becomes operative and a vicious cycle is established. If an individual has a good, realistic self-image, this leads to successful operations and a benevolent instead of a vicious cycle is established.

What an individual needs to develop properly is a realistic, positively oriented self-image. The extremes of an overly negative or overly positive self-image must be avoided. The overly negative self-image is seen in the self-image of the typical drinking alcoholic. The drinking alcoholic, largely as a result of the biases and ignorance of society, tends to view himself as a hopeless moral degenerate instead of as an individual with a disease which, like diabetes, can be successfully handled. In the instance of the drinking alcoholic, an enlightened understanding of the nature of alcoholism can bring about a transformation of self-image in the direction of greater realism and accuracy; and this change can lead to a lasting sobriety and an ever deepening healed and enlightened state of consciousness. The overly positive self-image is seen in the self-images proposed and espoused by certain Eastern and Western philosophically and/or religiously oriented groups. In Christian Science, for example, the individual is taught to have an image of himself or herself as being here and now "immortal, perfect, wholly good, untouched and untainted by evil because man expresses God."[16] In the view of Christian Science, sin, sickness, suffering, and death are illusions and cannot really touch the individual. In my view these aspects of the self-image which Christian Science inculcates are false and can harm the individual in his growth to the extent that man's true condition and his grave responsibility in the molding of his eternal character and destiny are obscured or misinterpreted. In spite of what I think are certain erroneous aspects of the self-image that Christian Science proposes, it is to be praised for its stress on the need to overcome ignorance and on the reality of the spiritual healing power of God-given understanding.

What is necessary then for the individual is to strive for a realistic self-image which is neither excessively negative nor overly positive and to operate out of this self-image. There are always gaps between the self as it is and the image the individual has of the self. There will always be a gap between the self one presently happens to be and the self one is called to become, and this entails an inevitable gap between the image one has of the present self and the "ideal-image" one has of the self one hopes to become. Besides the image of the perfect self one is ultimately summoned to become, there is also the image I have today of the self I hope to become tomorrow. This latter self-image is of necessity ideal, since it is of a self that is not yet realized, but if it is to function fruitfully, it must be realistically scaled down to a proximately realizable ideal. This type of ideal self-image is the one that can be effectively realized within a determinate period of time.

A constant transformation in self-image is as natural and essential to the individual as the growth of the self. The process of human maturation involves a continuous transformation in both self and self-image. Of course, transformation in self-image is a highly subtle matter and is first and last the gracious work of God, presupposing always our free response to his metamorphosing, healing initiative. Unfortunately, bookstores abound in unintentionally deceptive, incredibly facile and naïve positive-thinking-oriented books which promise a perfect self overnight and thus lead to disillusionment rather than authentic transformation.

The issues of self-image and transformation in self-image

are vital in the process of maturation in Christ, and the achievement, active reception of, wholeness and self-transcendence. If authentic transformation in self-image is to be realized, the process must be viewed and carried out within the total ambit of the healing-through-enlightenment reality.

Selves and Transformations: Final Thoughts

Meditation on these "selves" and their characteristics can play a very important and salutary, healing role in the elimination of distortions in self-image and the development of a richer, more authentic and positively oriented self-image. Christian revelation offers the individual a self-image which is at once realistic and yet full of hope and radically optimistic. True enough, authentic Christianity acknowledges the reality and gravity of the facts of original and personal sin. Yet at the same time, the whole point of the Good News of Jesus Christ is that where sin abounded grace is in yet greater abundance. If Christian revelation requires of the believer that he acknowledge his sinfulness, at the same time it proclaims the healing of man through the powerful grace of Jesus Christ. The Christian, though he is called to acknowledge his weakness, is told that he is to make the words of the apostle Paul his own: "There is nothing I cannot master with the help of the One who gives me strength" (Philippians 4:13). The incredibly Good News of Christianity is that through the mercy of the Father the believer is enabled in a mysterious but real fashion to put on the mind of Christ and to have as his own that self-image which was also in Christ Jesus. "I live now not with my own life but with the life of Christ who lives in me" (Galatians 2:20).

NOTES

1. Thomas Hora, *In Quest of Wholeness*, ed. Jan Linthorst (Garden Grove, Calif.: Christian Counseling Service, Inc., 1972), p. 64.

2. Karl Rahner, "Grace," *Sacramentum Mundi* (New York: Herder and Herder, 1968), II,.p. 420.

3. Harold Greenwald, *Decision Therapy* (New York: Peter H. Wyden, 1973), p. 5.

4. Gerard Manley Hopkins, *God's Grandeur*, line 10.

5. Cited by John C. H. Wu, *Chinese Humanism and Christian Spirituality* (New York: St. John's University Press, 1965), p. 21.

6. Cited by M. Eugene Boylan, *This Tremendous Lover* (Westminster, Md.: Newman, 1947), p. 353.

7. Bernard Lonergan, *Collection* (New York: Herder and Herder, 1967), p. 250.

8. *Ibid.*

9. William Johnston, *The Still Point* (New York: Fordham University Press, 1970), p. 182.

10. Cited by Peter Kreeft, "Zen Buddhism and Christianity: An Experiment in Comparative Religion," *Journal of Ecumenical Studies* VIII (1971): 532.

11. Maxwell Maltz, *Psycho-Cybernetics* (New York: Simon and Schuster, 1960).

12. Cecil Osborne, *The Art of Understanding Yourself* (Grand Rapids, Mich.: Zondervan Books, 1967), p. 161.

13. Maxwell Maltz, *The Magic Power of Self-Image Psychology* (Englewood Cliffs, N.J.: Prentice-Hall, 1967), pp. 2–3.

14. Bernard Lonergan, *Method in Theology* (New York: Seabury Press, 1972), p. 30.

15. *Ibid.*

16. Leo Rosten, *Religions in America* (New York: Simon and Schuster, 1963), p. 40.

IV

Mind-Fasting and Spirit-Feasting

CHRISTOTHERAPY IS CONCERNED with the healing that comes through the light of Christ as meaning and value incarnate. Mind-fasting and spirit-feasting are existential techniques of Christotherapy. They are techniques because they are methods of actively receiving varied gifts of healing through enlightenment. They are existential because they are not artificial or arbitrary, but arise dynamically and naturally out of man's basic openness and graced call toward wholeness and enlightened holiness.

The expression mind-fasting, which Thomas Merton speaks of as the "fasting of the heart," is derived from Chuang Tzu, one of the greatest Taoist writers. Thomas Hora makes a creative use of mind-fasting as a technique in his existential psychotherapy. Spirit-feasting is an expression I have coined to serve as a positive complement to mind-fasting as I understand and develop this latter notion. In this book the techniques of mind-fasting and spirit-feasting are developed and applied within a specifically Christian context. Scripture provides certain grounds for a technique of "mind-fasting" in which the negative is overcome, and for a type of "spirit-feasting" through which the positive gifts of enlightenment are actively received.

73

Some other views, both ancient and modern, give primacy to the transformation of mind and heart in the healing process. A brief discussion of these views will serve to introduce the notions of mind-fasting and spirit-feasting.

The great Buddhist work the *Dhammapada*, for example, begins by telling us:

All that we are is the result of what we have thought: it is founded on our thoughts, it is made up of our thoughts. If a man speaks or acts with an evil thought, pain follows him, as the wheel follows the foot of the ox that draws the carriage.

. . . [But] if a man speaks or acts with a pure thought, happiness follows him, like a shadow that never leaves him.[1]

For the Buddha, it was through enlightenment or knowledge and the practice of four basic truths that man achieved "salvation." He taught that there was an eightfold path leading to enlightenment, and that the first two stages in the path, significantly enough, were "right knowing" and "right aspiration" or "right intention." Healing was above all a matter of transforming the mind and heart, freeing the mind from error and ignorance and the heart from false desires and values. At the heart of the Buddha's teaching, then, there is a call—though it is not named as such—for fasting of the mind and heart from all that is illusory, ignorant, deceptive and evil, and feasting of the spirit in "right knowing" and ultimately in the nirvana of eternal bliss.

Taoism, like Buddhism, places great emphasis on interiority and the liberation of the mind and heart. According to Chuang Tzu, the goal of mind-fasting or "fasting of the heart" is the achievement of an inner unity; for this it is necessary to empty the mind of pseudo-knowledge, preoccupation with the self, and distractions of the senses. In Chuang Tzu's words, "Fasting of the heart empties the faculties, frees you from limitation and from preoccupation. Fasting of the heart begets unity and freedom."[2] In this articulation of mind-fasting, there is a negative moment in which the person empties his heart and mind of all pseudo-knowledge and concerns, but the final emptiness achieved is very rich indeed:

Look at this window: it is nothing but a hole in the wall, but because of it the whole room is full of light. So when the faculties are empty, the heart is full of light. Being full of light it becomes an influence by which others are secretly transformed.[3]

Thomas Hora, following Chuang Tzu, envisages mind-fasting as a process which helps to make possible "hearing with the spirit." For Hora, mind-fasting is a cognitive form of prayer, a type of meditation which requires a continuous process of mental purification. The meditation that is mind-fasting involves a constant turning away of the mind and heart from erroneous assumptions and concerns and misdirected orientations. The goal is existential worship, through which one exists in union with God as the source of harmony, peace, and love. Mind-fasting is then a stage of cognitive prayer which is preparatory to spiritual prayer and existential worship. A person who worships existentially is in harmony with Love-Intelligence, and is reverential to the will of God, to existence, and to the fundamental order of being. Such a person manifests himself or herself to the world as a loving, free, harmonious, intelligent, wise, and beneficial presence.

From a purely secular perspective, Dr. Albert Ellis, in his rational-emotive psychotherapy, agrees with the religious thinkers on the importance of mental transformation in the healing process. The key insight in Ellis's therapy is that a person's emotional states are largely dependent on his thinking, and that emotional disturbances arise when individuals either consciously or unconsciously reiterate to themselves negative, unrealistic, illogical, self-defeating thoughts.

In his chief work, *Reason and Emotion in Psychotherapy*, Ellis points out eleven major irrational ideas which he finds rather common place in our culture, and which often lead persons who hold one or more of them into various forms of emotional illness or neurosis.[4] Among these irrational ideas are: (1) the idea that it is necessary for an adult to be loved or approved by every significant person in the community; (2) the idea that one must be completely competent in all possible respects in order to be worthwhile; (3) the idea that it is awful and catastrophic when things are not the way one wants them; (4) the idea that human unhappiness is externally caused, and that one has little or no control over sorrows and disturbances; (5) the idea that it is easier to avoid the difficulties and responsibilities of life than to face them. The goal of rational therapy is to bring the emotionally disturbed person to an understanding of the irrationality of ideas such as these that he may be reiterating to himself, so that he can be helped to dislodge these ideas from his consciousness and affirm internally more positive, rational ideas about life. In this way, emotional disturbances may be healed. Clearly there is an element of mind-fasting and spirit-feasting in Ellis's approach, since there is a need to discover and then put off certain false mental attitudes and to put on a more positive, rational mentality.

As techniques of Christotherapy, mind-fasting and spirit-feasting differ in varying degrees from the emphasis in the mental practices of Buddhism, Taoism, Ellis, and Hora. We should now consider mind-fasting and spirit-feasting from a Christotherapeutic viewpoint.

The apostle Paul points out in his second letter to the Corinthians that "for anyone who is in Christ, there is a new creation" (2 Corinthians 5:17). The Christian becomes a "new man" in Christ; while retaining its individuality, the self is gradually transformed into the Christ-self and comes to share "the divine nature" more deeply (2 Peter 1:4). The transformation of the natural self into the Christ-self entails the gift of a new mind and a new heart. Mind-fasting and spirit-feasting are graced operations which lead up to and are fulfilled within the lifelong process of transformation into the Christ-self and active reception of the gifts of the Christ-mind and the Christ-heart.

This process of transformation is multifaceted; it is a process of conversion on the intellectual, moral, religious, and psychological levels, involving participation and growth in various forms of enlightenment. It is a matter of constant self-transcendence, of a graced passage from raw potentiality to ever-higher levels of self-realization and self-fulfillment. As existential techniques, mind-fasting and spirit-feasting are at work on all levels of the process leading from the continual dying to the antiself and the anti-Christ-self, to the full realization of the self and the Christ-self. Mind-fasting is closely connected with the form of enlightenment called existential diagnosis, and spirit-feasting is associated with existential discernment—and more profoundly, with those forms of enlightenment and prayer which center on and delight in the positive and are nourished by the true, the good, the worthwhile, the beautiful, and the divine.

In what follows I will consider in turn (1) mind-fasting and spirit-feasting as existential techniques which can be grounded in Scripture; (2) the prayerful process that initiates and culminates mind-fasting; (3) some inauthentic and authentic modes of thinking, desiring, feeling, and being-in-the-world; (4) counterfeit and genuine forms of prayerful being-in-the-world. Inevitably, these will be closely interrelated.

Mind-Fasting and Spirit-Feasting as Grounded in Scripture

The author of Ephesians writes:

You must give up your old way of life; you must put aside your old self, which gets corrupted by following illusory desires. Your mind must be renewed by a spiritual revolution so that you can put on the new self that has been created in God's way, in the goodness and holiness of truth.

Ephesians 4:22-24

In this passage, the need for a certain mind-fasting and spirit-feasting is incipiently indicated. There is a need for a spiritual revolution, a radical renewal of mind, and this requires death to the old illusory desires of the self, and coming alive to the holiness of truth.

The call for mind-fasting and spirit-feasting can be grounded in the Hebrew Testament stress on transformation of mind and heart in religious conversion, but more proximately in Jesus' teachings concerning interiority and inwardness. From the beginning of his ministry, Jesus taught about the need for a *metanoia*, a conversion of mind and heart, which required repudiation of the old ways and faith in the Good News (Mark 1:15). In the simple "repent and believe the Good News," there is a seminal disclosure of the need for a type of mind-fasting and spirit-feasting.

Throughout his public life, Jesus stressed that inward thoughts and desires are critical in a person's growth or decline. According to the Gospel of Mark, Jesus said:

It is what comes out of a man that makes him unclean. For it is from within, from men's hearts, that evil intentions emerge: fornication, theft, murder, adultery, avarice, malice, deceit, indecency, envy, slander, pride, folly. All these evil things come from within and make a man unclean.

Mark 7:20-23

Again in Matthew, the crucial significance of a person's thinking and intentions is brought out when Jesus says: "You have learnt how it was said: You must not commit adultery. But I say this to you: if a man looks at a woman lustfully, he has already committed adultery with her in his heart" (Matthew 5:27f.). For Jesus, as for the Buddha and Chuang Tzu, the central issue is the thinking and desiring of the human heart. Man is capable of wrong thinking and right thinking, of inauthentic desiring and intending and of authentic desiring and intending. Jesus' view on the utter primacy of thought and desire in the process of salvation is nowhere more beautifully expressed than in his metaphor of the eye as the lamp of the body:

The lamp of the body is the eye. It follows that if your eye is sound, your whole body will be filled with light. But if your eye is diseased, your whole body will be all darkness. If then, the light inside you is darkness what darkness that will be.

Matthew 6:22f.

It is essential, for Jesus, for a person to dispel darkness and have an inward eye full of light, and this is the core meaning of mind-fasting and spirit-feasting as I employ these expressions.

In the various epistles, Jesus' teaching on the need for a transformation of mind and heart is expanded in the light of the postresurrection experiences of the Church. Jesus taught that conversion is a matter of becoming like a little child again, and the epistles abound in metaphors and expressions for the new life of a Christian. For example, the Christian is dead to the old self but alive for God in Jesus Christ (Romans 6:6-11). Again, in place of the old self there is the new spiritual self (1 Corinthians 2:14-15). Instead of the "old yeast of evil and wickedness" there is the "unleavened bread of sincerity and truth" (1 Corinthians 5:7-8). The new being in Christ described in the epistles in-

volves a certain type of mind-fasting and spirit-feasting.
Christians are to have minds "trained by practice to distinguish between good and bad" (Hebrews 5:14). The Christian is to put off the carnal mind which is at enmity with
God (Romans 8:7) and to put on the mind of Christ (Philippians 2:4). The Colossians are told to let their thoughts be
"on heavenly things not on the things that are on earth"
(Colossians 3:2), and Paul admonishes the Romans: "Do not
model yourselves on the behaviour of the world around
you, but let your behavior change, modelled by your new
mind" (Romans 12:2).

There are many other texts in Scripture which tell us
about the "two-edged sword" of enlightenment that I refer
to as mind-fasting and spirit-feasting. Indeed, these notions
are implicit throughout the epistles. There are two texts
which highlight particularly well what I mean by these
ideas. The idea behind mind-fasting is expressed forcefully
and clearly in this statement of Paul's:

We live in the flesh, of course, but the muscles that we fight with
are not flesh. Our war is not fought with weapons of flesh, yet
they are strong enough, in God's cause, to demolish fortresses.
We demolish sophistries, and the arrogance that tries to resist the
knowledge of God; every thought is our prisoner, captured and
brought into obedience to Christ.

                                        2 Corinthians 10:3-5

Mind-fasting cleanses the mind of all forms of "mental pol-
lution" and brings every thought into obedience to Jesus
Christ. Through it, the individual strips away the mask
from all false knowledge and reveals it as virulent ignorance
and falsehood. Mind-fasting is a weapon of the spirit, and
through the powerful aid of God's enlightening grace, it
drives out the dark and inauthentic thoughts from the temple of the spirit and prepares the way for the feasting of the
spirit at the banquet of wisdom. Perhaps no text in Scrip-

ture brings out more beautifully the rich and positive concept of a certain spirit-feasting than these words of Paul from the fourth chapter of Philippians:

> I want you to be happy, always happy in the Lord. . . . There is no need to worry; but if there is anything you need, pray for it, asking God for it with prayer and thanksgiving, and that peace of God, which is so much greater than we can understand, will guard your hearts and your thoughts, in Christ Jesus. Finally, brothers, fill your minds . . . with everything that is good and pure, everything that we love and honour, and everything that can be thought virtuous and worthy of praise. . . . Then the God of peace will be with you.
>
> Philippians 4:4-9

Spirit-feasting is practiced by anyone who is joined to the Lord and is one spirit with him (1 Corinthians 6:17). The individual who spirit-feasts dines at the banquet prepared by Wisdom. In Isaiah it was prophesied: "On this mountain, Yahweh Sabaoth will prepare for all peoples a banquet of rich food, a banquet of fine wines. . . . That day it will be said: See, this is our God in whom we hoped for salvation" (Isaiah 25:6-9). Spirit-feasting is living on every word that comes forth from the mouth of God (Matthew 4:4). Jesus used the image of a feast to describe the joys of the Kingdom, and the one who spirit-feasts eats and drinks at the table of Wisdom and says in thankful song to the Lord of the banquet: "You prepare a table before me. . . . you anoint my head with oil, my cup brims over" (Psalm 23:5). Spirit-feasting occurs on many levels, from a thankful delight in the beauties of sunrise and sunset to the intense joys of mystical marriage as described by Teresa and John of the Cross. Without the positive complement of spirit-feasting, mind-fasting would be sterile and dangerous in the vacuum it leaves; together, they are a powerful instrument for healing through enlightenment, sharper than any two-edged sword.

The Prayerful Process of Mind-Fasting

The aim of mind-fasting is to cleanse the mind and heart
of all inauthentic thinking, desiring, imagining, and feeling,
as far as this is possible, and God grants it. But in order to
mind-fast effectively, it is first necessary to recognize just
what inauthentic thinking and desiring are and why they
are inauthentic.

Throughout the Hebrew and New Testaments constant
stress is put on the illusory, deceptive quality of all thinking
and desiring that sets itself against the deepest orientations
of the true self and God. Eve blamed her transgression of
the divine command on the deception of the serpent. John
speaks of the devil as "a liar and the father of lies" (John
8:44). The author of Ephesians speaks of the "old self,
which gets corrupted following illusory desires" (Ephesians
4:22), and Paul writes in Romans of those whose "empty
minds were darkened" and who gave up "divine truth for a
lie" which made nonsense of reason (Romans 1:21-25). Inauthentic thinking and desiring, then, are always in some
way a matter of ignorance, darkness, and delusion.

Of course, not all ignorance of authentic meaning and
value is due to personal malice and sinfulness, though it is
always illusory, tragic, and a source of pain and disharmony. A far worse form of ignorance is the active, aggres-
sive ignoring of true value and meaning, which enthrones
the idol of the lie in the very sanctuary of truth. According
to the author of Ephesians, these individuals, the willing
victims of ignorance, are intellectually in the dark, "es-
tranged from the life of God, without knowledge because
they have shut their hearts to it" (Ephesians 4:18). In their
utter blindness, they exalt their ignorance as the truth, and
so they are above all in need of healing through enlightenment. As the *Tao* puts it, "to regard our ignorance as knowledge, this is mental sickness. Only when we are sick of
sickness shall we cease to be sick."[5]

It is clear from scriptural revelation that the darkened, ignorant, deluded mind and heart of man is at the center of all disharmonies and that healing and salvation are a matter of dispelling darkness and filling with light. Mind-fasting appears as a primary existential tool of the healing process. Yet, to mind-fast effectively, one must unmask the ignorant thought and illusory desire and reveal them for what they are, and this is difficult because pseudo-knowledge and false values disguise themselves as true wisdom and authentic value. Evil is made to appear good and the false true. It is necessary to take captive every thought and desire and bring them as prisoners before Christ to see if they can stand irradiated by his pure light. This is precisely the approach recommended in Ephesians:

> Try to discover what the Lord wants of you, having nothing to do with the futile works of darkness but exposing them by contrast. The things which are done in secret are things that people are ashamed even to speak of; but anything exposed by the light will be illuminated and anything illuminated turns into light.
>
> Ephesians 5:10-14

The author of this text is urging that certain sexual practices and attitudes be subjected to scrutiny in the clear light of Christ and revealed for what they are: the worship of a false god. Here we have an instance of a key element in the process of mind-fasting.

More specifically, the prayerful process of mind-fasting may be expressed in four basic stages: (1) experience; (2) reflective prayer, or the prayer for understanding; (3) revelation; (4) demonstration. Though they are closely interrelated, it will be helpful to consider each in turn.

A first clue to the possible need for mind-fasting may be found in the *experience* of a disease, accident, or disharmony on some level of existence, whether physical, mental, moral, psychological, or spiritual. Just as from a secular viewpoint Ellis sees an emotional disorder as a sign of irra-

tional beliefs in the diseased person, so Christotherapy sees
any disharmony in a person as a call to self-transcendence,
and very possibly as a symptom of the presence of inauthentic thinking and desiring.

The second stage of the prayerful process of mind-fasting
is *reflective prayer* or the *prayer for understanding*. In Christotherapy every experience, including the experience of
internally—or externally—manifested disharmonies, has
valuable meaning for the one who has eyes to see and an
open heart. Often enough, a disease is a symptom of a
misdirected, existentially ignorant mode of thinking, desiring, and feeling-in-the-world. Once the proper meaning of
the disease is understood and the erroneous thinking corrected, the disharmony or disease vanishes. Reflective
prayer, the prayer for understanding, is a dynamic expression of the mind and heart desiring to understand the existential significance of an experience of disharmony. The
prayer of the existentially reflective man is not so much
"What should I do, Lord?" as "What should I know,
Lord?" or, even more simply, "Lord, grant that I may see!"

On the level of reflective prayer the attitudes of humbleness of heart, listening, *wu wei*, and letting-be should be
present as deeply as possible. This is because the mind and
heart are very much subject to the seductive sway of illu-
ory thought and desire. As it is expressed in Titus, "To all
who are pure themselves, everything is pure; but to those
who have been corrupted and lack faith, nothing can be
pure—the corruption is both in their minds and in their
consciences" (Titus 1:15). It is essential, then, for the person who would receive the gift of a revelation of healing-
meaning to exist in a state of obediential receptivity, of
choiceless awareness, of letting-be, so that the experience
may yield up its meaning just as it truly is.

In the third stage, then, there is the gift of understanding
of the existential meaning of an experience, and this is *reve-*

lation. If the experienced disharmony or disease was a symptom of inauthentic thinking and desiring, the person's revelation will be an insight into it, an existential diagnosis of the inauthentic thinking and desiring. For example, an individual with an ulcer may come to understand or existentially diagnose that his ulcer is the symptom of an excessively ambitious mental and affective striving. Examples could be multiplied indefinitely. The basic insight, however, is that in the prayerful process of mind-fasting, the moment of revelation is the graced understanding of the inauthentic thinking and desiring and feeling that underlie an experience of disharmony.

The fourth stage, the moment of *demonstration*, is the actual living-out of the insight received on the level of revelation. The demonstration, for example, which flows from a person's insight into the existential meaning of his ulcer could be a constant mind-fasting from all forms of excessively ambitious desiring and striving. If the revelation was correct and the mind-fasting is properly carried out together with spirit-feasting (we prescind from this positive element for the moment), the ulcer should vanish and a state of harmonious integration should be achieved. These, then, are the four stages of mind-fasting.

To avoid certain possible misunderstandings, a few points should be made about the overall process of mind-fasting. First, not all experiences of disharmony on some level of existence are symptoms of the presence of inauthentic thinking and desiring in a person. They may, indeed, be the expression of a need for growth or for a vocational change, or for a deepening in understanding and self-transcendence in some area of a person's existence. This means that the revelation which comes as the result of the prayer for understanding will not always be a matter of existential diagnosis. It may involve existential discernment, a graced understanding of a new vocational call, or a deeper insight into the unsearchable mystery of one's participation in the death and resurrection of Christ. Again, the revelation may be a certain divine silence and a call to bow in adoration before the mystery of God in his transcendence. Man has no right or need to demand an explanation of God. The revelation which Job received is an example of this; he was given an understanding that God is the transcendent mysterious one who cannot be called to account but who contains within his heart the explanation of all pain and sorrow. In the face of a Joblike experience of God, the silence of loving adoration and total confidence is the only response.

Second, the revelation one receives need not be a special illumination such as Paul received on the road to Damascus. For the most part, God in his providence makes use of our own powers of reasoning and discerning, and the revelation we receive comes through our own mental processes guided by the light of grace. Still, everything that man is and thinks and does is a gift, and so every revelation is in a profound sense more the work of God than of man.

Third, in the prayerful process of mind-fasting God expects his servants to use all the helps he has provided. This means that participation in the sacramental life of the church and consultation with the enlightened ones of God are important factors in existential diagnosis and discernment, as well as in demonstration. Also, because there is an element of human fallibility in every person's thinking, we must always be conscious in our practice of mind-fasting that we are weak, and work out our salvation with humility, reverence, and awe.

Finally, though it is true that not all illnesses and disharmonies are the result of inauthentic thinking and desiring, it is a brutal fact of life that very many are. Existential diagnosis and mind-fasting are consequently extremely effective and important existential methods for actively receiving healing through enlightenment. If, instead of rushing to the medicine cabinet or to the physician at the first symptom or pain, more individuals were to engage in prayerful mind-fasting, there might be a considerable increase in the number of enlightened healings and a considerable decrease in the need for pills and medical consultation.

The Gates of Hell and the Gates of Paradise

GATES OF HELL	GATES OF PARADISE
Sensualism	Perceptivity
Emotionalism	Understanding
Possessivism	Letting-Being-Be
Intellectualism	Wisdom
Personism	God and Man in God

Jesus sometimes used the imagery of "ways" and "gates" in depicting the journey of man toward perdition or salvation. In the Acts of the Apostles, Christians are spoken of as followers of a "way." The ancient Christian work the *Didache* begins with these words: "There are two Ways: a Way of Life and a Way of Death, and the difference between these two Ways is great."[6]

Now just as there are many kinds of error but truth is one, so the number of possible gates or ways to destruction is infinite but the ways of life all coalesce into one: the love of God with all one's heart and soul and mind and strength and of all others in God. The heaven and hell spoken of here refer not only to the final eternal state of man's consciousness, but also to the internal state of man's consciousness here and now. For, as Jesus pointed out, the kingdom of God and the kingdom of Satan are present realities. As the Buddhist *Dhammapada* puts it:

The evil-doer suffers in this world, and he suffers in the next; he suffers in both. He suffers when he thinks of the evil he has done; he suffers more when going on the evil path.

The virtuous man is happy in this world, and he is happy in the next; he is happy in both. He is happy when he thinks of the good he has done; he is still more happy when going on the good path. [7]

The various gates of hell and gates of paradise refer respectively to certain fundamentally inauthentic and authentic modes of thinking, desiring and doing in the world. The description of salient characteristics of these gates is intended to be a help for the prayerful process of mind-fasting and the joys of spirit-feasting. Much of the phenomenological analysis of these ways of inauthentic and authentic existence is taken immediately from the writings of Thomas Hora, and nuanced and further developed in the light of Christotherapeutic principles.

Sensualism. The sensualist way of being-in-the-world is basically concerned with the pursuit of pleasure and the avoidance of pain, with feeling good and avoiding feeling bad at all costs. Desire and fear, rather than authentic meaning and value, are the motivating forces in the life of the sensualist. He is self-indulgent and hedonistically inclined. Sex, for the sensualist, is masturbatory, and personal beauty is reduced to the sphere of eroticism. The sensualist tends to have an "alimentary approach" to life: he takes in or spits out, he immediately likes or dislikes, and accepts or rejects in terms of his likes and dislikes.

The sensualist is a subjectivist, and the world is his "apple pie." He tends to interpret all things in terms of how they make him feel, and is therefore constantly misinterpreting; whatever he experiences undergoes a process of adulteration. He is diseased, tragically blinded to the realm of the spirit, and subject to a number of ailments because of this. With his "alimentary" view of things, the sensualist often suffers from various gastrointestinal difficulties. His excessive concern with feeling frequently expresses itself in emotional upsets, hysterical outbursts, and sometimes in severe hypochondriasis. The radical solution to the problems of the sensualist is complete transformation in consciousness and a shift of emphasis from feeling good to being good, and to putting on the Christ-consciousness.

Perceptivity. To be perceptive is to be completely open, in one's sense and spirit, to reality as it truly is. Where the sensualist subordinates being good to feeling good and views reality through the jaundiced eye of his distorted sensibility and subjectivity, the perceptivist pursues authentic value, makes goodness his primary concern, and uses his senses in the quest for true meaning and value. The perceptivist feels good because he is good. He is converted morally, loving and appreciating true value; intellectually, acknowledging the reality and primacy of spirit; and religiously, submitting lovingly to the Absolute. And so, a radical transformation has taken place in his sensibility. The perceptivist is capable of the most exquisite aesthetic experience because of the presence in him of moral, intellectual, and religious conversion, which open the gates of his senses to beauty and all the splendor of aesthetic form shining in the sense object. He enjoys the richest form of sense experience because all of his sensing is metamorphosed by spirit. So, for him, the act of love in authentic wedded union is at its peak moments a most ecstatic experience of inspirited, divinized sensitivity. The sensualist, however, is blinded to this whole world of spiritualized sensitivity. Paul says, "The unspiritual are interested only in what is unspiritual, but the spiritual are interested in spiritual things. It is death to limit oneself to what is unspiritual; life and peace can only come with concern for the spiritual" (Romans 8:5-6).

Emotionalism. The emotionalist mode of being-in-the-world is a more subtle form of sensualism. The emotionalist is ruled by his feelings, rather than by understanding; he has spontaneous likes and dislikes and acts according to them. He is thus a reactor, and not a responder. Tending to be affected in his actions, the emotionalist is often a sentimentalist. Frequently his life is characterized by a quest for excitement. A whole host of disturbances of a somatic and emotional character flow from the emotionalist's mode of being-in-the-world.

Understanding. The gate of paradise opposed to emotionalism is expressed in the precept "Be understanding." To be understanding is not to be without feeling, but rather, to possess that true self-knowledge and knowledge of others from which authentic feelings naturally arise. Jesus provided an example of the relationship which should exist between emotions and understanding when he wept over Jerusalem. As always, Jesus' tears were genuine, flowing from a true understanding and loving concern for men and the human condition.

Possessivism. The possessivist individual is one who is ceaselessly covetous, dominated by the desire to have. Possession, rather than the gift of joy, intoxicates the mind of the possessivist. His desire to have can cover a wide range of possibilities. He may seek to have material objects, to have a personality, to have people, even to have a religion. This attitude covers the whole range of materialism, as well as those who act for the sake of acting. The possessivist is the victim of the illusion that having is more fulfilling of human life than actively receiving the gifts of God. In his desire to have, the possessivist becomes possessed; he ends up "being had." No one ever clings to a gift in the gracious presence of the giver; this is to defile and desecrate the act of giving. Authentic having flows from gracious receiving, but the possessivist subordinates authentic being to having, and so he really has nothing at all. What he clings to takes hold of him and dominates his consciousness like an idol.

Letting-Being-Be. This is the gate of paradise, the authentic state of consciousness, that alone makes possible a fruitful and lasting form of having. Man's fundamental act is to let Being or God fulfill him. His calling is to let God's Kingdom come within him. Jesus told us to pray, "May your name be held holy, your kingdom come, your will be done" (Matthew 6:9f.). It is by letting God be God for him that a man comes to have and possess in a true sense. Christ promised that those who were primarily concerned with the coming of the Kingdom of God would have all other things added as well (Matthew 6:33). The way, then, to have in an authentic manner is to say "Amen" to God, to let-Being-be. Any attempt to put having before letting-Being-be is doomed to failure, and there will be no real having at all. In this case, "from the man who has not, even what he has will be taken away" (Mark 4:25).

Intellectualism. There is a way of knowing that leads to life and wholeness, but there is another way that leads to death, and this is the gate of hell called intellectualism. The intellectualist seeks self-gratification and self-glorification through his possession of knowledge. He looks at knowledge as "my" knowledge, "my" theory, "my" hypothesis. Through the possession of knowledge, the intellectualist seeks to have power over others. At an intellectualist gathering of scholars the participants come ostensibly to listen and learn, but actually to be listened to and to be praised and extolled for mental excellence. Because of the pride he takes in his knowledge, the intellectualist finds it very difficult to admit mistakes. He is biased and calculating and so misinterprets data in terms of his own assumptions and beliefs and cherished ideas. The intellectualist is one of the so-called wise and learned of this world to whom the mysteries of the Kingdom are not revealed (Matthew 11:25). Paul referred to the intellectualist when he spoke of the knowledge that gives "self-importance" (1 Corinthians 8:1) and of "the arrogance that tries to resist the knowledge of God" (2 Corinthians 10:5). Thomas Hora has learned in

his practice of psychotherapy that the calculating, analyzing, objectivizing, dissecting individual can be subject to
many forms of mental illness, and that his children especially may suffer everything from hyper-self-consciousness
and loss of spontaneity to catatonic rigidity and paranoid
schizophrenia. Perhaps even more than the sensualist, the
intellectualist is in need of the healing light of the Christ-
meaning and the Christ-value.

Wisdom. The gate of paradise opposed to the intellectualist gate of hell is wisdom. The individual wise in Christ
understands himself to be a created expression of Love-
Intelligence, a transparency through which the divine light
may shine, an instrument of God, a manifestation of creative Wisdom. For him, every insight is a gift to be shared
unselfishly with others. The truly loving and wise man
understands that what is freely received is to be freely given
and shared with others. He is unbiased, open to all that is,
since he sees himself called to respond to the truth, to bear
witness to the truth, and to let the truth shine through him
so that the Father may be glorified. It is of this loving
knowledge, this wisdom, that Solomon spoke:

And so I prayed, and understanding was given to me;
I entreated, and the spirit of Wisdom came to me.
I esteemed her more than sceptres and thrones;
compared with her, I held riches as nothing. . . .
I loved her more than health or beauty,
preferred her to the light,
since her radiance never sleeps.
In her company all good things came to me,
at her hands riches not to be numbered.

                                        Wisdom 7:7-8, 10-11

Personism or Person-olatry. All the gates of hell involve
forms of idolatry. The sensualist and emotionalist make
idols of the feelings. The possessivist turns having into an
idol. The intellectualist makes idols of his schemes, ideas,

and hypotheses. The personist is an individual who ab-
solutizes the self or other human selves. Current trends in
psychology, philosophy, and religion which stress that man
and not God is the center and master of things are engaged
in person-olatry. Hora writes of the personist mentality in
his statement, "Self-centered consciousness does not discern the Ground of Being. Interpersonal consciousness is
focused on the interaction of the self and the other. It fails
to see that background without which the foreground could
not appear. The interpersonal focus ignores the truth of
what really is."[8] The personist sees himself or other human
beings as the only source of hope and love and light in the
world. The personist mentality is echoed in its tragic implications in Matthew Arnold's *Dover Beach:*

Ah, love, let us be true
To one another! For the world, which seems
To lie before us like a land of dreams,
So various, so beautiful, so new,
Hath really neither joy, nor love, nor light,
Nor certitude, nor peace, nor help for pain. . . .[9]

Person-olatry, like all other forms of idolatry, is deluded,
ignorant, darkened, and diseased, and can be healed only
through an existential acknowledgment of the transcendent
God in whom all things subsist and have their being.

God and Man in God, or Radical Monotheism. The gate of
paradise opposed to personism is radical monotheism,[10]
which is the explicit existential acknowledgment that God
alone is Absolute and that all created things are to be valued
and judged and loved in the light of the Love-Intelligence in
which they have their being. For the radical monotheist, a
loving and worshipful observance of the first commandment is just as important today as it was in the time of
Moses. The radical monotheist sees that the love of man is
inseparably conjoined with the love of God, but adores

God alone and knows that it is only through the Spirit's gift of love in his heart that he can love others with fidelity, perseverance, self-sacrifice, and true commitment. He acknowledges that God gives the gift of his love even to those who have no explicit knowledge of him but are men of good will. At the same time, the radical monotheist resolutely maintains that as long as a person does not explicitly adore the Father of Jesus Christ he is in a state of existential ignorance and needs greater healing through enlightenment.

These considerations of the various gates of hell and of paradise are not intended to be exhaustive, but simply to suggest basic forms of inauthentic and authentic thinking, desiring and acting in the world. In the concrete individual, there is often a blending of various inauthentic forms of thinking and desiring so that each particular case requires its own peculiar existential diagnosis.

Each of the gates of hell and gates of paradise may hold true for a society as well as for an individual. A family or a society or a nation can be just as dominated by a sensual attitude toward existence as any individual can be. Sociologist Pitirim Sorokin spoke of whole cultures as basically sensual in their interests. Even brief reflection will show that families, groups, and nations can become obsessed with the desire to possess rather than to seek true values such as universal liberty and justice. The ideology of a group or society or state may correspond to the intellectualism of an individual. Finally, fanatical racist and nationalist movements can correspond to the personist gate of hell.

The gates of hell have their societal dimensions; in large measure, the attitudes and value-systems of individuals are shaped by the larger forces around them. Parents, for example, greatly determine the values of their children, and society may greatly determine the thinking and valuing of its members in the same way. Thomas Hora has written that human values are mostly imposed on a person in his formative years by his environment. It follows that man may not be responsible for having acquired wrong values; but it is his responsibility to try to uncover these wrong values and change them when they are found, adopting healthy values.

Today men exist in a "noosphere," a climate of thought that encompasses the whole world. Through the different media, we are constantly bombarded with "messages" about how to think and desire and feel. Many of these messages are basically inauthentic, and yet often enough they are received and accepted without conscious advertence. The mental atmosphere becomes increasingly polluted and harmful, and can be the source of "diseases" of every kind. Injustice itself is a disease in all of its oppressive forms, racism, domination of the poor by the rich. Urgently needed is existential diagnosis on the societal, as well as the individual, level. Families and nations must reflect together on the values of life-meanings they hold dear, and through prayerful reflection come to understand what is inauthentic in their collective beliefs and assumptions, and then with God's help move forward in mind-fasting and spirit-feasting.

I do not mean to imply that personal sin may not be at the heart of various problems and sicknesses, both of particular persons and of groups. But I want to emphasize that often unconscious existential ignorance lies at the core of these problems, and the healer or therapist must be careful not to increase someone's guilt feelings when he should be an instrument for healing through enlightenment.

The key point to be kept in mind in our consideration of the prayerful process of mind-fasting is that much of the suffering and disease that persons face in their lives is a direct symptom and consequence of misdirected concerns,

erroneous assumptions and beliefs, and inauthentic thinking and desiring. Healing comes to a person when his false
mental and affective attitudes are lost and new, more positive concerns are found. It is never enough, though, simply
to ignore or repress false mental attitudes. First, they must
be seen and unmasked. Once they are understood to be
inauthentic they lose their attraction and can be eliminated
through mind-fasting. Of course, the inauthentic mental
content, images, beliefs, and assumptions that are eliminated must be replaced by positive concerns; simple elim-
nation will not suffice. Thus, for every gate of hell re-
nounced there must be a gate of paradise found. Above all,
it is through constant contemplation of the Christ in his
mysteries and participation in the Christ through his sacraments and love of the Christ in one's neighbors that the
True Way to Paradise, in all its richness, is found.

Inauthentic and Authentic Forms of Prayer

Mind-fasting, in its prayer for understanding, and
spirit-feasting, in its core moments, are prayer in the strict
and proper sense, so it is appropriate to end this chapter
with a discussion of prayer. Unfortunately, like every other
human activity, prayer can be inauthentic as well as authentic, and so we must first examine certain general forms
of inauthentic prayer before discussing the key forms of
true prayer.

INAUTHENTIC FORMS OF PRAYER

The inauthentic prayer modes we will briefly consider,
based largely on Hora's writings, are sensuous and
emotionalist prayer, possessivist prayer, intellectualist
prayer, ritualist prayer, and personist prayer.

Sensualist and emotionalist prayer are self-indulgent forms of prayer in which the desire to feel good masquerades as piety. Sensual-emotionalist prayer appears at times in certain types of religiously oriented sensitivity sessions, in some primitive revival groups, and in exaggerated forms of Catholic devotionalism. Extremes of this type of prayer are the various masochistic or sadistic mascerations of the flesh done in the name of religion, which are actually emotional hysteria. In general, whenever feeling good rather than being good becomes the primary focus in prayer, inauthenticity is involved. Thus, the author of *The Imitation of Christ* pointed out long ago that what should be sought in prayer is primarily the God of all consolation rather than the consolation of God. Of course, nothing is wrong with consolation; it is a gift of God. But it should be the flowering and fruit of an authentic being-in-the-world and an enlightened consciousness.

The prayer of the possessivist is dominated by the desire to have rather than to be. God infallibly answers all prayers for growth, for a fuller existence, for greater healing through enlightenment, but the possessivist wants to have some finite "object." He demands of God a job or a spouse or money or a certain kind of success, not realizing that at the core of all prayer there must be a thirst for righteousness and a humble acknowledgement that God alone knows what is best for the individual. In his self-centered blindness, the possessivist often asks God for something that would harm him. Of course, as a loving Father, God will never give a poisonous snake to his child, no matter how hard the child begs. The possessivist must learn that all prayers of petition must have as their underlying thrust a desire for enlightened holiness, and that all requests for specific objects should be expressed conditionally. Jesus gave the example of how we should address prayers of petition to the Father when he prayed in the garden the night before he was crucified: "My Father . . . if it is possible, let this cup pass me by. Nevertheless, let it be as you, not I, would have it" (Matthew 26:39).

The prayer of the intellectualist is boastful and self-righteous. It is concerned with outer show rather than inner spirit, loving to display its intelligence. Intellectualist prayer prides itself on its elegance of expression; it is a kind of mental vanity and indulges in verbiage and pretty phrases. The intellectualist in his prayer thanks God that he is not weak and sinful like the rest of men. His prayer is centered on the self and self-expression rather than on God and God-glorification.

Another type of inauthentic prayer is "ritualistic prayer." I place the term in quotation marks because there are certain ritual prayers which are authentic. These are inspirited ritual prayers, prayers with a heart and a soul. Such, for example is the Eucharistic prayer when properly carried out. Unfortunately, there are also many inauthentic "ritualistic" prayers, which may be motivated by fearful, superstitious, magical thinking. This is the kind of prayer found in some primitivist cults and in many contemporary revivals of witchcraft, devil-worship, and the black arts. Nor are Christians always free of superstitious prayer. Prayer is "ritualistic" if it is motivated by hypocrisy or social conformism. In this, the individual's lack of true piety and holiness may be disguised as "pious" participation in public prayer ceremonies and religious services. Christ denounced the prayer of the hypocrite in the most scathing terms: "Alas for you, scribes and Pharisees, you hypocrites! You who are like whitewashed tombs that look handsome on the outside, but inside are full of dead men's bones and every kind of corruption. In the same way you appear to people from the outside like good honest men, but inside you are full of hypocrisy and lawlessness" (Matthew 23:27-28).

Personist prayer means all forms of prayer which concentrate exclusively on self-expression or on interpersonal relationships. Individuals dominated by a personist mentality regarding prayer see it solely as a means of self-articulation or of deepening interhuman relationships. All mention of God is deliberately excluded from the prayer of the personist, and the whole reality and meaning of prayer is horizontalized and reduced to the sphere of the human. Christians should engage in existential diagnosis of their own manner of praying to discover whether their prayer is the prayer of Abraham, Isaac, and Jacob, the prayer of Jesus the Christ and his apostles and saints, or whether it is the emasculated pseudo-prayer devised by certain clever but unenlightened contemporaries.

It has been necessary in the context of mind-fasting and spirit-feasting to discuss various forms of inauthentic prayer because there is so much unfortunate ignorance today about the true nature of prayer, and consequently there is a great need for healing through enlightenment in this vital area. It is in the deepest aspirations of a person's prayer that his true state of consciousness is revealed. An individual prays for what he treasures most, and where a person's treasure is there you will also find his heart and the god he truly serves. If a person's prayer is radically sensualist, his secret god is revealed to be the self and its feelings; if a person's prayer is intellectualist at its core, the secret deity inhabitating the inner shrine of his heart is seen to be his own ideas and ambitions. And so it goes. Therefore, existential diagnosis can be a very useful instrument of healing through enlightenment for one who suspects or detects areas of inauthenticity in his fundamental prayer life.

AUTHENTIC PRAYER

All authentic praying, whether one realizes it or not, is an encounter with God the Father through the mediation of his Son Jesus in the power of the Holy Spirit. Thus all authentic prayer is a communion in love and knowledge and desire with the Love-Intelligence that is revealed in the Christ-event as Father, Son, and Holy Spirit. Inspired individuals have used countless ways to describe the phenomenon of prayer, but all of them can be summed up as a dialogic encounter of man with his God.

In this brief discussion of authentic praying I examine some key characteristics of prayer within the explicitly Christian context of loving communion with the Father through his Son Jesus Christ in the power of the Spirit. Prayer may be spoken of as Spirit-and-spirit-feasting, and as existential worship, under the forms of repentance, petition, praise, and thanksgiving, all of which bring a constant deepening in healing and enlightenment. I think all authentic prayer can be summed up in a mantra which the person who seeks healing through enlightenment may most fruitfully use: Abba, Amen, Alleluia.

All authentic praying is Spirit-and-spirit-feasting. Everyone who prays authentically prays in the Spirit and "in spirit and truth" (John 4:24). All authentic prayer is first of all and most radically a gift, and a gift through the Spirit of Christ imparted to the human spirit. Without the gracious presence and aid of the Spirit, it is impossible even to say, "Jesus is Lord" (1 Corinthians 12:3). Through the Spirit alone we are able to cry out, "Abba, Father" (Romans 8:16). Paul tells us that "the Spirit himself and our spirit bear united witness that we are children of God" (Romans 8:16). In our weakness the Spirit comes to our assistance and "expresses our plea in a way that could never be put into words" (Romans 8:26). Paul adds that "God who knows everything in our hearts knows perfectly well what he [the Spirit] means, and that the pleas of the saints expressed by the Spirit are according to the mind of God" (Romans 8:27). All prayer is Spirit-and-spirit-feasting because all authentic praying is inspired in man's spirit by the

Spirit of Christ. It is feasting because to hear the word of God is to be nourished by Wisdom itself, and all Spirit-inspired prayer is first of all the whispering of the inner secrets of the divine Lover within the human heart.

Authentic prayer may be spoken of as existential worship. Spirit-inspired prayer ultimately addresses God, adores him, and acknowledges him as the ground of all that is and the radical source of healing and life, and this is the meaning of worship. Moreover, authentic praying is *existential* worship because it is never abstract but always concrete, in tune with one or other vital areas of human existence, individual as well as social.

It is important to stress the reality of authentic praying as existential worship because the radical meaning of the incarnation is that God loves and concerns himself with all that man is and does, and with every atom of the universe in which man exists. This means that in all praying, God is speaking to man about what concretely concerns him, and man's response must always be in terms of the concrete. There is no room in authentic prayer for an isolated I-Thou relationship which prescinds completely from other human beings and the cosmos in which man lives. This is why Ignatius of Loyola crowns his *Spiritual Exercises* with "The Contemplation for Obtaining Love," in which he invites the retreatant to behold God lovingly at work in all creation; in response to his vision of the divine Lover at work, the retreatant is to bend all the energies of his heart toward loving, worshiping, and serving God. Each one of the specific forms of prayer is a loving act of existential worship.

The prayer of repentance is existential worship because it is a loving sorrow for past offenses against God, a turning toward God with trust in his mercy and forgiveness, and a firm resolve to be in the future a true friend and son or daughter, ever more faithful to the sweet exigencies of the self and the Christ-self. The prayer of repentance is the prayer of the pilgrim, the prayer of each Christian as long as he journeys in this life. All authentic repentance is Spirit-inspired, love-filled, God-centered, and so a profound expression of existential worship.

Another form of existential worship is the prayer of petition. Through it, the one who asks acknowledges his total dependence on God and expresses a loving trust in the guiding providence of the Father who gives all good things to his children. Jesus urged his followers to pray the prayer of petition, to do so again and again even with importunity, to persevere, to ask with the assurance that the prayer will be answered. The one who authentically prays the prayer of petition knows that it is the Spirit deep within him who is praying to the Father for what the person truly needs for growth and life. For this reason the petitioner can pray with confidence, knowing that because it is the Spirit who is groaning within him, the prayer is already answered in the saying of it.

The prayer of petition has not become outmoded. It was used constantly in the Hebrew Testament period; it was urged by Jesus, by his disciples and evangelists, and by the authors of the epistles. It has been a constant practice throughout the tradition of the Christian Church. Misunderstanding of the prayer of petition arises when it is seen as a work of man rather than of the Spirit. If the prayer of petition is seen as an effort to bribe God or to change God, then it is misunderstood and should not be practiced. But if it, like all other authentic forms of prayer, is seen primarily as the work of the Spirit of God bringing about a change in the consciousness of man, then it is an excellent form of existential worship.

Prayers of praise, thanksgiving, and joyful adoration are the richest forms of existential worship, and pertain not only to man's life as a pilgrim here on earth, but to his glorious resurrected state of everlasting indwelling in the New Jerusalem. Prayers of repentance and petition will fade away, but the prayers of thanksgiving, praise, and song-filled adoration will resound through eternity at the Marriage Feast of the Lamb, where Spirit-feasting will reach its peak in everlasting spiritual bridal ecstasy.

Love is at the heart of the existential worship of praise, thanksgiving, and adoration. This means that even here on earth, through the experience of these forms of prayer —above all in the Eucharistic banquet and in mystical moments—man enjoys a foretaste of the joys of the resurrection to come. To dwell in love is the source of all joy, and love in its most basic, eternal form—delight in the true, the good, the beautiful and the worthwhile—is the wellspring of all praise, thanksgiving, and adoration. Praise and adoration are thus the joyous, rapturous expression of the delighted spirit in the presence of goodness and beauty. Within God's eternity it is out of delight in his own infinite goodness and beauty and fullness of light and life that his *agape*, his desire to communicate his goodness, is born. In the same way, it is out of the internal experience of the gift of God's love flooding one's heart and of the new kingdom of value which faith—the eye of love—discerns, that delight and praise and thanksgiving arise in the human heart and overflow in a desire to share the Good News with every creature. These are the nature and the effects of the existential worship which is expressed in prayers of praise, thanksgiving, and song-filled adoration.

In the discussion of healing through enlightenment, authentic prayer must be seen as an intense form of and participation in the enlightenment that heals. All forms of authentic prayer are a participation in healing through enlightenment because prayer is a communion in knowledge and love with the Three Who are One God, and love and knowledge shared between lover and beloved are the most pow-

erful healing forces the world has known. Robert Ochs, in a
beautiful little book entitled *God Is More Present than You
Think*, [11] stresses the point that prayer is an opening of one's
mind and heart to the divine Lover who speaks to us in our
own thoughts and desires. God is constantly in dialogue
with the human person in his thoughts and desires; recognition of God speaking within one's own spirit should become
an ever-deepening source of healing and light. Prayer, then,
is a matter of listening for the "still, small voice" of the
divine lover deep within the mind and heart, and of re-
sponding with joy when the voice is heard. The poet Hopkins writes, "I greet him the days I meet him and bless
when I understand."[12] This might be taken as a motto by
every true seeker of healing and enlightenment through
prayer.

To end this discussion of authentic prayer, I would like
to suggest the words "Abba, Amen, Alleluia" as a "Christian mantra" to be used in prayer. Jesus himself used these
three words, and they can serve to remind the one who
prays of the essentially trinitarian nature of Christian
prayer.

The word *abba*, as we have seen, is the Hebrew diminutive meaning "daddy." Jesus used it to address his Father
and he told us that we too should dare to address the Father
in this intimate term. John writes, "Think of the love the
Father has lavished on us, / by letting us be called God's
children" (1 John 3:1). One might humbly adapt John's
words and say, "Think of the love the Father has lavished
on us, by letting us call him Abba, Daddy."[13]

Amen is a word which Jesus often used, and it means "it is
true." In the language of today we might say, "Let it be."
Let God be God. Let the Father be our Father. Let Jesus be
our elder brother! Let the Father transform us into the
image of his Son! In the book of Revelation Jesus is called
"The Amen" (Revelation 3:14), the one who is faithful and

true. Jesus is the Amen of the Father because the Father was the center of his consciousness and he did whatever he saw the Father doing. Jesus' love for mankind was born out of his love for the Father. We are called to be transformed into Jesus, to have his consciousness, to become other Christs. It is our high vocation to make the Abba the center of our consciousness. Amen, then, is not only the name of our elder brother, it is our own deepest name. We are called to become ever more totally Amens to the Father. So be it then. Amen.

Alleluia is a Hebrew word which means "Praise Yahweh." It is through the Spirit of Christ that we are able to praise God with joyous and ecstatic hearts. Alleluia echoes throughout the liturgies of the Church, above all in the seasons of Easter and Pentecost. Though Scripture does not use it as such, then, Alleluia is a most fitting word for the Holy Spirit. The feast of the Spirit resounds with Alleluias; he is indeed the love, the ecstasy, the joy of the Father and the Son, and our love and joy and consolation as well. It is through the Spirit alone that we are able to say "Abba" and "Lord Jesus," and there is no greater cause for joy, praise, and thanksgiving than to be able to say those blessed words. It is through the power of the Spirit that Alleluias well up within our hearts and the Spirit himself is our Alleluia. The book of Revelation tells us that Alleluia is sung at the Marriage Feast of the Lamb, and that it is the Spirit who says, "Come." All creation joins together in one great Alleluia Chorus. The word "Alleluia," then, is the expression of the joy of spirit-feasting at its deepest level, and one of the richest forms of existential worship.

It is then most fitting that the prayer of the Christian be expressed in these three words: Abba, Amen, Alleluia!

NOTES

1. *The Wisdom of China and India*, ed. Lin Yutang (New York: Modern Library, 1955), p. 327.

2. Thomas Merton, *The Way of Chuang Tzu* (New York: New Directions Publishing Corporation, 1965), p. 53.

3. *Ibid.*

4. Albert Ellis, *Reason and Emotion in Psychotherapy* (New York: Lyle Stuart, 1971), pp. 60–88.

5. John C. H. Wu, *Chinese Humanism and Christian Spirituality*, (New York: St. John's University Press, 1965), p. 87.

6. *Early Christian Writings*, trans. Maxwell Staniforth (Baltimore: Penguin Books, 1968), p. 277.

7. *The Wisdom of China and India*, p. 328.

8. Thomas Hora, *In Quest of Wholeness*, ed. Jan Linthorst (Garden Grove, Calif.: Christian Counseling Service, Inc., 1972), p. 50.

9. Matthew Arnold, *Dover Beach*, lines 29–34.

10. H. Richard Niebuhr, *Radical Monotheism and Western Civilization* (Lincoln: University of Nebraska, 1960), p. 34.

11. Robert Ochs, *God Is More Present than You Think* (New York: Paulist Press, 1970).

12. Gerard Manley Hopkins, *The Wreck of the Deutschland*, p. 5.

13. John Navone, *A Theology of Failure* (New York: Paulist Press, 1974), pp. 110–114, presents Hora's understanding of the healing power of ceaseless prayer. The author believes that Hora's affirmations "generally corroborate, from the standpoint of psychiatry, our theological reflections on the healing character of our participation in the 'Abba' relationship of Jesus, that dynamic relationship radically transforming those who accept it." I might add that if an individual prefers to address the God of Jesus Christ as Mother or "Mama" rather than as Father or "Daddy" I see no fundamental theological difficulty here, since the First Person of the Trinity is, in fact, neither male nor female. I, however, do not see it as necessary to go "beyond God the Father" for a new primal divine name and so retain the masculine name in the present book.

V

The Mysterious Law of Death and Resurrection

A KEY ELEMENT of the Good News is that Jesus Christ provides a way for us to be victorious conquerors in our struggle with sickness, suffering, and death. Jesus came above all to save us from our sins, but an essential element in his saving work was showing us a way and giving us the inward power to come to grips effectively with all the consequences of sin. Among these consequences are sickness, suffering, and death.

Bernard Lonergan has written of "the mysterious and just law of the cross,"[1] and a brief consideration of this mysterious law will give us a good starting point for the discussions in this chapter. Reflecting on the meaning of the redemption, Lonergan discerns a process consisting of three stages in what he calls "the law of the cross." The stages are: (1) sin and the punishments which result from sin; (2) the voluntary transformation of the punishments or effects of sin into a certain good; and (3) the blessing given this transformation by God the Father.

The law of the cross operates first in Jesus, and then through Jesus in all those who freely choose to follow him and let the law of the cross work within them. Jesus freely, and yet out of obedience to the Father, takes upon himself certain effects of sin, that is, suffering and death, even though he is innocent of all sin. Through his voluntary acceptance of suffering and death, Jesus triumphs over these evils and makes them stepping stones to salvation. Finally, the Father blesses the work of his Son, and because Jesus became obedient even to death on the cross, the Father raises him up and glorifies him, making him the principle of salvation for all who accept and follow him.

There are certain differences, as well as similarities, between the way the law of the cross is at work in Jesus and in the rest of mankind. Basically, Jesus *redeems* through his participation in the law of the cross, while all others *are redeemed* by letting the law work within them. Moreover, while Jesus in his complete innocence freely allows himself to experience the effects of sin, the rest of mankind is called to acknowledge its sinfulness, to accept freely the punishments which flow from sin in a spirit of repentance and hope in Christ, and in this way to participate in his victory. The Father calls all of us to become like his beloved Son and to suffer and die with him so that we may be resurrected and glorified with him. "If in union with Christ we have imitated his death, we shall also imitate him in his resurrection" (Romans 6:5).

Through the mysterious and just law of the cross, the Father chose to bring good out of evil and to conquer Satan and the empire of sin by turning the effects of sin into a means for moral and religious self-transcendence. For the followers of Christ, then, sickness, suffering, and death need not be the cause of bitterness, dark hatred, and despair but, rather, an opportunity for growth in hope and in love, for healing through enlightenment of the highest order. Through his insight into man's participation in Christ's victory over suffering and death, Francis of Assisi was able to praise "Brother Fire" when it cauterized his flesh and to sing in his *Canticle of Brother Sun*: "Be praised, my Lord, in our Sister Bodily Death."

The law of the cross is a profound expression of the mystery of the redemption, but there is considerable nuancing needed in the development of the law if the individual who seeks healing through enlightenment in the midst of sickness, suffering, and death is to find the particular healing meaning he most needs. Though all disorders in the universe of man have their ultimate root in the original and personal sinfulness of mankind, there are many different proximate explanations for the particular disorders individuals experience in their lives. In the next section of this chapter I will consider from an existential viewpoint some proximate explanations for the sickness or sufferings or deaths that individuals may undergo. The chapter will end with reflections on Jesus' attitude toward his own suffering and death—an attitude all are called to share—and on the mysterious "joy in suffering" which should characterize the enlightened Christian.

Some Concrete Modes of Suffering in This World

One common form of suffering is the type which results from deliberately doing evil. Of this the author of the first epistle of Peter was speaking when he wrote: "There is nothing meritorious in taking a beating patiently if you have done something wrong to deserve it" (1 Peter 2:20). Suffering that results from deliberately doing evil may be externally inflicted or it may come in a mental or physical illness, or emotional anguish. The suffering that results from personal sinfulness is useless to the sufferer unless it becomes the occasion of repentance. Paul speaks of the suffering that leads to repentance as "a kind of suffering that God approves" (2 Corinthians 7:9), and he contrasts it with the useless suffering of the worldling: "To suffer in God's way means changing for the better and leaves no regrets, but to suffer as the world knows suffering brings death" (2 Corinthians 7:10). All evil thinking, desiring, and doing inevitably bring in their wake some disharmony, some mode of suffering, and unless this suffering is used as an occasion for repentance it breeds further discord, worse sin, and ultimately death. "Don't delude yourself into thinking God can be cheated: where a man sows, there he reaps: if he sows in the field of self-indulgence he will get a harvest of corruption out of it" (Galatians 6:7-8).

Another source of great suffering is existential ignorance: that is, ignorance of certain vital meanings and values necessary for wholeness in spirit, mind, and body. Everyone is to some extent existentially ignorant, not necessarily because of any personal fault, but simply as a result of his membership in the sinful race of Adam. The children of sensualist-emotionalist parents may inherit the inauthentic life-understanding and values of their parents, for example, and so suffer the disharmonies which flow from such a mode of being-in-the-world. The irrational ideas which Albert Ellis sees as the root sources of various emotional disturbances are grounded in existential ignorance. Unfortunately, these irrational ideas are widely held and bring great suffering to many people.

Happily, there is an antidote to the many forms of existential ignorance and it is the medicine that is Jesus Christ. In the teachings of Jesus, in the Sermon on the Mount and elsewhere, inauthentic modes of being and irrational ideas about how to live are exposed for what they are, and the true way to think and be-in-the-world is revealed. Jesus, in his being and his teaching, conquers existential ignorance and, through participation in his healing light and way, all men are called to share in his victory.

Besides the suffering that comes from personal sin and

existential ignorance, there are other sufferings that come to man simply as the price of membership in the sinful race of Adam. Concupiscence, man's inability to concentrate sin-glemindedly on the pursuit of the truly good, causes much suffering. So do the sickness and frailty which remind man of the inevitability of death. Such suffering involves all that flows from the mounting surd of man's collective sinfulness and the evil effects this has in individual lives, in groups, and in the whole race. Finally, the suffering which flows from participation in the human condition includes so-called "accidents" and natural upheavals. Nature itself is affected for the worse by individuals' sins and bears the scars of man's original and collective sinfulness.

Just as the suffering that results from personal sin can become an opportunity for self-transcendence and sincere repentance, and just as the suffering that flows from exis-tential ignorance can provide an occasion for healing through enlightenment, the sufferings that come to man as a result of the human condition can become important op-portunities for growth if they are handled in the right way. By the mysterious wisdom of the cross God enables human persons to use every kind of suffering as an occasion for transformation and self-transcendence. As the apostle Paul expressed it, "We know that by turning everything to their good God cooperates with all those who love him" (Romans 8:28).

Regarding suffering which man experiences as a result of what theologians call concupiscence, there is present a defi-nite call to self-transcendence and healing. In the experi-ence of concupiscence an individual is summoned by God to accept his human nature with its limitations and at the same time to acknowledge gratefully the reality and power-ful presence of Christ's healing and enlightening grace. The experience of weakness can become an occasion for glorying in the strength of God. Paul wrote to the Romans, "What a wretched man I am! Who will rescue me from this body doomed to death? Thanks be to God through Jesus Christ our Lord!" (Romans 7:24).

In the illnesses that come to an individual as a result of his sharing in the human condition there is always present a call to transcendence. Christ opposed illness and rebuked it as a sign of the reign of Satan and of sin in the world. The follower of Christ, in the same way, is to have the mind of Christ toward illnesses and to try to eliminate sicknesses from the world to the extent that he can. If an individual is sick because of his own sinfulness he should combat the empire of sickness by repenting of his sins. Again, if an individual is ill because of some form of existential igno-rance he should try to overcome the illness through the prayerful process of mind-fasting and existential diagnosis.

If a person's illness does not seem to be the result of personal sin or existential ignorance, this still does not mean that the sickness should be passively endured as some mys-terious "gift of God." Instead, the person should actively oppose the sickness and take whatever enlightened means he can to be free of it. This includes prayer and espe-cially the anointing of the sick and participation in the Eucharistic sacrificial banquet. If the gift of full healing does not come, even after constant prayer and the reception of the sacraments, the individual should trust that the light and power of Christ's healing grace are always available to him, so that even in the throes of his sickness he can be a sign of Christ's victory by manifesting a hopeful serenity and self-transcendence.

A stoical resignation and passive endurance in the face of sickness is never the authentic, enlightened Christian re-sponse. Christ viewed sickness as an enemy to be con-quered, and the follower of Christ is called not to succumb passively to sickness but to overcome and to transcend it in whatever enlightened way he can. There is, of course, some sickness that leads to death, and there a special attitude is required, but this issue will be best handled in our discussion of Christ's death and its message and meaning for the dying Christian.

In this discussion of the sufferings that flow from man's human condition and his concrete situation in the world, something should be said about so-called "accidents." An accident in the common usage of the word is an event that occurs by chance, apart from any intention, design, or intelligibility. Everyone is subject to unanticipated painful happenings but the attitude a person takes toward these so-called accidents will in large measure determine the quality of his sufferings. A person who looks upon accidents as matters of pure chance with no meaning behind them will respond with dread, fear, stoic impassivity, or, at best, the resolve to make the best of a bad situation. The poet William Ernest Henley in his *Invictus* provides an example of proud stoic resolve in the face of chance:

In the fell clutch of circumstance
I have not winced nor cried aloud.
Under the bludgeonings of chance
My heart is bloody, but unbowed.[2]

From another perspective, though, which I believe is the correct one, there is no such thing as an "accident." Such a view was expressed eloquently by Carl G. Jung just a few days before his death:

To this day God is the name by which I designate all things which cross my willful path violently and recklessly, all things which upset my subjective views, plans and intentions and change the course of my life for better or worse.[3]

Jung is here naming what most men call accident or chance "God." He is not identifying God with chance, but he is saying that the so-called chance event is not arbitrary at all,

but full of the meaning and transcendent wisdom of providence.

Jung's view seems to be in profound accord with Hebrew
and New Testament teachings. In the book of Wisdom it is
said of the wisdom of God: "She deploys her strength from
one end of the earth to the other, / ordering all things for
good" (Wisdom 8:1). Jesus constantly stressed the need to
become as little children, confidently trusting in the Abba
who seeks only good for his little ones, numbers the very
hairs of the head, and guides the flight of the sparrow. It
was trust in the loving providence at work in all things
which enabled the psalmist to say: "Though I pass through
a gloomy valley, / I fear no harm; / beside me your rod and
your staff / are there, to hearten me" (Psalm 23:4).

For the Christian seeker of healing through enlightenment, then, the "accident" is not a surd in a universe of
blind happenings but a meaningful event and a call to self-
transcendence. Sometimes an accident is a summons to renounce some conscious or hidden sinful way of being-in-
the-world; sometimes it is a call to unmask a form of existential ignorance; sometimes it is a revelation of a new vocation or direction to follow; sometimes an accident is an
invitation to grow in loving adoration of the mystery that
guides all things lovingly and wisely but often leaves
human beings baffled and confused. Such was the case of
Job when, at the end of all his trials and in the moment of
his enlightenment, he said:

I am the man who obscured your designs
with my empty-headed words.
I have been holding forth on matters I cannot understand,
on marvels beyond me and my knowledge. . . .
I knew you then only by hearsay;
but now, having seen you with my own eyes,
I retract all I have said,
and in dust and ashes I repent.

                                                    Job 42:3, 5-6

Besides the various forms of suffering discussed so far, there is also suffering involved in the growth process—what we often call "growing pains." Because of man's original and personal sinfulness, there is a type of suffering involved in growing which would not be present if man had not sinned. It is not possible to say what the human growing process would have been if sin had not entered the world. There might have been a certain natural "tension" involved in man's growing process even in a sinless world. But then the tension might have been purely ecstatic in nature, like the tension that immediately precedes a great discovery or arises in the act of love. Now, though, there is a suffering involved in man's growing which is the result of original sinfulness but which, properly used, can lead to ever richer growth and maturation on all levels of human existence. Existential diagnosis is necessary in the presence of the tensions and sufferings related to growth in order to understand what is holding one back in the maturation process, and positive enlightenment is required to discern ever richer ways of growing to full maturity in the self and the Christ-self.

Psychiatrist Kazimierz Dabrowski has elaborated the notion of "positive disintegration"[4] to explain the process of psychic maturation; this concept is a useful tool for practicing existential diagnosis in one's psychic growth generally, and especially in regard to such fundamental growth transformations as moral, intellectual, and religious conversion.

In Dabrowski's analysis a positive kind of disintegration is needed for reaching high-level maturity. This process of positive disintegration involves the dissolution of lower-level functions and structures so that a higher level of integration can be achieved. There is an initial, primitive stage of integration and functioning which must be dissolved so that a new, richer integration can be achieved. According to Dabrowski the movement of positive disintegration is often heralded by disquietude with the self, feelings of inferior-

ity, experiences of shame and guilt, environmental malad-
justments, and various psychoneurotic conflicts. In his
view these so-called negative experiences can have a very
positive function and are signs of the need for a disintegration or dying to a present level of being and functioning-in-
the-world, so that a new and higher level of integrated
being-in-the-world may be found.

From the viewpoint of Christotherapy, Dabrowski's notion of positive disintegration is very helpful in the application of existential diagnosis to the suffering and tension
involved in the growth process. Through existential diagnosis of disquietude, inferiority feelings, guilt, and so on, it
may be understood that there is a call to go beyond certain
learned but inadequate modes of being-in-the-world to
more authentic, higher-level modes of existence.

For example, it is possible to see positive disintegration at
work in the various stages of the passage from infancy to
adulthood, especially in moral, intellectual, and religious
conversion. Clearly, if a youth is to become a man he has to
give up the things of youth and take on the things of a man.
This passage almost invariably involves a crisis of disintegration, but if handled properly it will prove to be the positive disintegration that leads to authentic adulthood. Again,
stages are involved in moral development; and disquietude,
tension, and disintegration are required in order to move
from one stage to another. The same is true of the areas of
intellectual and religious development.

Lawrence Kohlberg of Harvard speaks of moral development in terms of six stages, grouped into three moral
levels.[5] First, there is the pre-moral level, where the child
operates according to the pleasure-pain, reward-punish-
ment principle. Second, there is the morality of conven-
tional role conformity: the child is good to avoid disap-
proval, and an individual obeys the law because society
requires it. Third, there is the morality of self-accepted
moral principles. The moral individual does what is mor-

ally right because his conscience tells him it is the right thing to do. Kohlberg points out that for a person to move from a lower to a higher stage of moral activity he must become dissatisfied and cognitively disturbed about the inadequacy of his present stage of moral activity. In other words, a positive disintegration should take place. Often what parents view as disobedience on the part of their teenage children is actually a stage of positive disintegration which is preliminary to the passage into authentic and religious conversion. In each of these forms of growth there is need for a dying to the old so that a higher mode of being may be born.

It is clear from this that suffering is involved in growing. The issue, then, is not whether an individual will experience tension and suffering in the growth process, but whether he will use these painful experiences in an enlightened way instead of allowing them to defeat him. For besides positive disintegration there is also negative disintegration in which one fails to come to grips in an authentic, enlightened way with the disintegrative elements in one's experience.

It is always necessary to seek an understanding of the underlying significance of one's experiences of disintegration in the process of growing. Existential diagnosis, not a flight from understanding, is the only authentic way to proceed. Flight is never a solution; it only results in a stunted, deformed psyche.

These insights of existential psychotherapy are in profound accord with the teachings of Christ, who told his followers to *take up* the cross and follow him (Matthew 10:38). This taking-up of the cross, in the terms of the psychology of growth, can mean a dynamic coming-to-grips in an enlightened fashion with the tensions and sufferings involved in growing, so that through dying to the old self a new and higher level of existence can be achieved. Paradoxically, the one who takes up the cross finds it a light

burden and a sweet yoke (Matthew 11:30) because it leads
to a higher form of existence. The one who refuses to take
up the cross, however, is crucified in spite of himself and
feels great pain and disharmony rather than the joy of
wholeness and mature integration.

There are still more forms and aspects of suffering to be
considered. There is, for example, the "suffering of the
just," which is the suffering that the righteous undergo
because of their righteousness. There is the mystery of
vicarious suffering, the suffering borne by one individual
for the sake of others. And, inevitably, there is the suffering
which comes in dying—a suffering all the sons and daughters of Adam are called to face. But, pervading all sufferings
metamorphosed in the light of Christ there is a radiant joy.
The joy present in suffering is one of the most striking
characteristics of the victory over sickness, suffering, and
death that men are offered in Jesus Christ.

We need to look at Christ in his suffering and dying for
an example of how best to face our own suffering and
death. For in everything that Christ said and did there is a
healing meaning, and this is above all true of his suffering
and dying. As the Abbott Marmion pointed out in his excellent work *Christ in His Mysteries*,[6] there are special gifts of
understanding connected with each of the mysteries of
Christ's life; and the Christian, by contemplating Christ in
his mysteries, may receive these special gifts of enlightenment and healing. Interestingly, it is in the context of a
hymn about Christ emptying himself and dying that Paul
urges the Philippians, and through them all of us, to have
the same mind that was in Christ Jesus (Philippians 2:5-11).

The Passion and Death of Jesus

The scriptural accounts of the passion and death of Jesus
differ in various ways and so there are disputes about what

is strictly historical in the accounts and what is the result of creative theological reflection on the part of the evangelists. It is impossible here to enter into these disputes. What we can say is that the composite scriptural account of Jesus' passion and death was written under the inspiration of the Spirit for those who would come to believe in Jesus as the Christ, so that they could understand the mind of Christ in his suffering and dying. This means that the Gospel accounts must be an authentic reflection, not a contradiction, of the way Jesus actually suffered and died. For example, if Jesus did not accept his suffering and death freely, and did not die confidently relying on the Father, then the scriptural accounts are useless and deceptive. In the same way, if Jesus in his suffering and dying was basically self-centered, only concerned about his own pain, rather than deeply interested in others and in obeying and trusting the Father, then the scriptural accounts are misleading and cannot help us to have the mind of Christ in our own suffering and dying.

The composite scriptural image of Jesus in his passion and death is of a man, a God-man, who suffers and dies but who does so freely, obediently, ecstatically—concerned about others and the Father rather than himself—and with a sense of triumph. The overall scriptural image of Jesus in his suffering and dying is of a person who in the very worst of circumstances did the very best of things.

Unfortunately, all through the history of the Christian Church, misunderstandings and errors have cropped up about the true nature of Jesus's suffering and dying, and these misinterpretations have led to tragic aberrations in spirituality and ascetical practices. A fixation on the sufferings and anguish of Jesus developed, which tended to overlook the beautiful self-transcendence and victory which he displayed in his passion and dying. Crucifixes that show Jesus writhing in agony and seemingly in despair epitomize this fixation on pain.

Some interpreters look on Jesus' cry on the cross—"My God, my God, why have you deserted me?" (Matthew 27:46)—as a despairing expression rather than the beginning of a prayer of confidence and victory. Most interpreters today, though, agree that Jesus' words are actually a quotation from Psalm 22, and this psalm is anything but a cry of despair. It is the prayer of a righteous sufferer who, despite his agony, trusts fully in God's loving protection and is completely confident that God will vindicate him.

In this context it is important to note the remark the centurion made immediately after Jesus died. As Mark records it, "The centurion, who was standing in front of him, had seen how he had died, and he said, 'In truth this man was a son of God'" (Mark 15:39). As a recent commentator has pointed out, it is clear from Mark's account that the centurion's remark was not based on the signs which followed Jesus' death, but on the close observation of the way that he died. We may say of a person that he "died like a man," but the centurion, after witnessing the way Jesus died, exclaimed, "He died like a son of God," like someone who was more than a man.

Keeping this in mind, the Greek crucifix which portrays Christ on the cross robed in splendor comes closer to showing the reality of the crucifixion than do some bloody Spanish crucifixes. Of course, the bloody crucifix does remind us that Jesus really did suffer and really did die, but it ignores the fact that in the very process of his suffering and dying Christ was truly a victor. John the evangelist was profoundly true to history when he called the passion the beginning of Jesus' hour of glory. In a book on the Good News of healing it cannot be stressed too much that Jesus was already victor in his suffering and dying, even before his resurrection, and in the same way he gives us the strength and inner light to be victorious in our suffering and dying.

The mysteries of Christ's passion and dying are inexhaustibly rich in their healing meaning, value, and power. Here, though, consideration can be given to only a few of the healing values and meanings present in the suffering and dying of the Lord.

One striking feature of Jesus' sufferings is that he never experienced the worst pain of all, that which flows from one's own personal sinfulness. Jesus was like us in all things except sin and, it should be added, the sufferings that flow from personal sin. The healing message in this for us is that there are many pains we can and should avoid in life simply by living righteously. There is no point to undergoing the sufferings that result from personal sin, yet all of us are sometimes vulnerable to this kind of suffering.

Another significant feature of Jesus' suffering and dying is that it was done in freedom and yet in perfect obedience to the Father. This means that Jesus did not view his suffering and dying as meaningless or as the result of some blind force or Fate. Jesus knew that the mysterious wisdom and loving providence of the Father was at work in his passion and dying and so he freely accepted it, trusted the Father, and triumphed in and through it. The healing meaning here is that for those who love and trust in God, suffering and dying cease to be unmitigated meaningless horrors and become instead opportunities for self-transcendence and victory.

Jesus was also very human in his passion and dying. It is natural for a man to seek wholeness on all levels of his being and to oppose disintegration, so it was natural for Jesus to experience intense revulsion and agony in the face of imminent physical torture and destruction. He was no masochist and he valued life tremendously. Knowing this, it is interesting to compare Jesus' attitude toward his passion and death with the reactions of many cancer victims as they come to grips with the malignancy of their condition.

Elizabeth Kubler-Ross, in her excellent book *On Death and Dying*,[7] speaks of five stages which many cancer victims go through on their way toward death. They are: (1) denial and isolation; (2) anger; (3) bargaining; (4) depression; and (5) acceptance. As his passion grew imminent, Jesus went through what is often called "the agony in the garden," as he experienced, in ways compatible with his sinlessness and divine person, an excruciating anguish in the face of crucifixion. Even though Scripture portrays Jesus earlier as yearning to consummate his saving work by suffering and dying, when he is confronted with it he asks the Father to spare him from it if possible. But once he knows it is the will of the Father, he moves toward suffering and death with calm and resolution. What often takes place over a long period of time in cancer victims as they come to terms with their own Golgotha was telescoped into a few hours in Jesus' agony. Jesus did not attempt to ignore the reality of his passion by radical denial, nor did he angrily blame God and cry out, "Why me?" as so many people do who know they are dying, but he did flinch in the face of his passion and experience fear and intense anguish of spirit; he did ask the Father to spare him if possible.

In the end, Jesus accepted freely the chalice of suffering and drank it, but first he went through a kind of inner experience that many cancer victims go through when confronted with imminent death. The healing meaning in the agony of Jesus is that it is very natural, not something to be ashamed of, to experience fear, depression, the desire to escape, and other anguishes of the spirit at the onslaught of intense suffering and certain death. But once the Father's will is clearly manifested, we are called to accept, and the gift of inner strength will be given to those who pray for it.

A further characteristic of Jesus' final suffering and dying is the ecstasy. I use the word "ecstatic" here in the literal Greek sense, which is "to stand outside oneself." Throughout the Gospel accounts of Jesus' suffering and dying, he is portrayed as a "man for others" and a "man for the Father." From the beginning of his "hour of glory" at the Last Supper until he handed over his spirit to his beloved Abba, Jesus' extraordinary concern for others was manifest.

As Jesus went forth from the garden, he healed the ear of the servant of his enemy. Although Peter had denied him three times, Jesus looked straight at him as he was led away. The mystics have referred to Jesus' look as his "loving glance," since it stirred deep repentance in Peter's heart. On the road to Calvary, Jesus turned to a group of women who were weeping for him and said: "Daughters of Jerusalem, do not weep for me; weep rather for yourselves and for your children" (Luke 23:28). His concern was for them, because he knew that the tragedy was not his, but theirs.

Jesus exercised his healing power even on the cross; to the thief who saw in him something to hope in, he said: "I promise you . . . today you will be with me in paradise" (Luke 23:43). To the very end Jesus was a faithful son and loving master, showing his deep filial piety by commending his mother to the care of his disciple John, and honoring John, whom he loved in a special and tender fashion, by giving him care over the greatest treasure he had on earth, his mother. Jesus showed the greatest concern for those who had brought him to his crucifixion, as he prayed, "Father, forgive them; they do not know what they are doing" (Luke 23:34). It would be difficult to find, in the whole history of mankind, a more splendid example of "ecstatic" suffering and dying than that of Jesus.

The source and inspiration of all that was ecstatic in Jesus' suffering and dying was the Father. As in his private and public life, so in his last pain and death, it was love of the Father that dominated the mind of Jesus. In the agony on the Mount of Olives, Jesus fled to the Father for guidance and strength, and the Father answered him: "An angel appeared to him, coming from heaven to give him strength" (Luke 22:43). God's care and presence are manifested all through the Hebrew and Old Testaments by his angels. On the cross, it was to the Father that Jesus prayed his victorious prayer from the 22nd Psalm, and in the end it was to his beloved Abba that Jesus committed himself: "Father, into your hands I commit my spirit" (Luke 23:46). The healing message for all who must suffer and die is that the Abba is the source of all one's strength, and he above all other things should occupy the mind of the sufferer.

Jesus' passion and dying shed light on two forms of suffering we have not yet considered: a suffering that results from living righteously in the world, and the vicarious suffering which is borne in the place of and for the sake of others. Both these forms of suffering were radically present in Jesus.

Jesus' suffering was a result of his living righteously in the world, his uncompromising adherence to dwelling in truth and justice. He was innocent and sinless, a source of light and healing for everyone who would open himself to him, but the forces of darkness and evil could not bear the light, and the full fury of their demonic powers was unleashed against him. He did not try to escape the assault of evil, but met his attackers head-on to atone for the sins of all mankind. This was his conquest.

The disciple is not above the master, and Jesus told his followers that they would be persecuted for their righteousness, just as he was. Yet he promised: "Happy are those who are persecuted in the cause of right: theirs is the kingdom of heaven" (Matthew 5:10). In persecution borne for a righteous cause, there is a kind of joy—not a masochistic delight in suffering or a "sick-soul" mentality, but a joy which flows from the realization that love of the Kingdom conquers all and no enemy can destroy love.

The disciple of Jesus is called to suffer for others just as he did. Man is social by nature, as we have seen, and this means that the sin of one individual touches all mankind. In the same way, the good deed of one person touches everyone else. Jesus suffered and died for all men as the new Adam, so that through him redemption could be won. As followers of Jesus, we are called to bear one another's burdens; sometimes this means suffering and dying for others so that they may be helped to live. Scripture stresses that "The heartfelt prayer of a good man works very powerfully" (James 5:16), and Paul writes in Colossians: "It makes me happy to suffer for you, as I am suffering now, and in my own body to do what I can to make up all that has still to be undergone by Christ for the sake of his body, the Church" (Colossians 1:24). Paul does not mean that he thinks his own sufferings increase the value of Christ's redeeming death, but that as a follower of Jesus he is called to share with him in his victory over suffering by triumphing in suffering.

In contemplating the sufferings of the righteous and the suffering borne for others, we must keep in mind that these flow from an intense love, and so they involve a deep-set joy. There is no greater expression of love than to suffer and die for others; from this love a great peace and blessedness of heart arise. Jesus said that all who suffered for the sake of righteousness would be happy, and there is a sense of accomplishment in such suffering which fills the spirit with great confidence and assurance. Jesus showed such an assurance of spirit when he finally said, "It is accomplished" (John 19:30).

It remains to reflect on the healing meaning in Jesus' death for all of us who must sooner or later die, and on the mysterious "joy in suffering" which seems to fill the followers of Jesus in the epistles and the Acts of the Apostles. But to understand these fully it will be helpful to examine

briefly the deaths of Buddha and Socrates and to compare
them to the death of Jesus.

The splendidly serene deaths of Buddha and Socrates are
often contrasted with Jesus' brutal and violent passion and
death. Dom Aelred Graham has written of the natural response of Buddhists to Jesus' death: "The depiction of an
almost naked human being nailed to the cross as an object to
be revered is unintelligible, with its presentation of barba-
rous cruelty, to a devout Buddhist, who is predisposed to
regard violent death in any form, as a result of bad karma."[8]
Graham also cites Karl Jaspers's comment on the way that
Socrates died: "The death of Socrates gives a picture of
serene composure in nonknowledge filled with ineffable
certainty." He adds his own comment, saying, "I wondered
if there was any better way to die."[9]

Outwardly, there are great contrasts between the deaths
of Buddha, Socrates, and Jesus. Buddha in some ancient
documents is depicted as dying amid serenity and beauty;
one account of his last hours states:

He lay down in the lion attitude on his right side and though it
was out of season, flowers fell from the sal tree in full bloom, and
covered his body. Divine mandarava flowers and sandalwood
powder fell from the sky and divine music and singing sounded
through the air in his honor.[10]

The contrast between the external circumstances of
Buddha's death as just described and Jesus' could not be
more pronounced. Buddha died amid flowers and music,
surrounded by his beloved disciples; Jesus died amid curs-
ing and jeering, nailed on a cross between two criminals.
There was a certain violence in Socrates's death, since he
drank hemlock, but like Buddha he died among his friends
and disciples in an atmosphere of great tranquillity. Contemplating these three men's deaths, there are few who
would not choose to die like Buddha.

But a full evaluation of the deaths of Buddha and Socrates requires further examination of the reasons why they died and their attitudes of mind and heart. Buddha died because after preaching his message of enlightenment it was necessary for him to lay aside his compound state and pass into nirvana. The last words attributed to Buddha are, "Now, then, monks, I address you; subject to decay are compound things: strive with earnestness." His state of mind was one of great enlightenment, but as he died he is said to have passed through ever-higher levels of enlightenment until he reached nirvana. Socrates's death was the result of his fidelity to conscience and the voice of wisdom which spoke within him. For the Socrates of Plato, all life was a process of learning how to die, because in death one is freed from imprisonment in the sense world, and the good and enlightened man goes to dwell in the realm of spirit and true life. Socrates was eager for death, since it meant to him a final liberation from the shackles of his body and a passage to the realm of the Forms of the Good, the One, and the Beautiful.

Jesus died because it was the way he could conquer sin and its effects, redeem mankind, and lead us to new life. As a Jew who valued the bodily integrity of man, Jesus did not view death as freedom from the cravings of the body, from illusions, or from imprisonment; rather, he saw it as a disintegration of the body which had to be accepted and transcended so that a higher integration of human existence could be achieved. In Jesus' dying there is a battle waged with the forces of darkness, and he fights as the new Adam, representing all of us, and through his suffering and dying he becomes the saviour of us all, our way to resurrection and newness of life.

It seems that Jesus' death will always be a scandal and a stumbling-block for many. As Paul wrote to the Corinthians:

. . . while the Jews demand miracles and the Greeks look for wisdom, here are we preaching a crucified Christ; to the Jews an obstacle that they cannot get over, to the pagans madness, but to those who have been called, whether they are Jews or Greeks, a Christ who is the power and the wisdom of God.

1 Corinthians 1:22-24

There seems to be a divine foolishness in the crucifixion, but Paul is quick to point out that "God's foolishness is wiser than human wisdom" (1 Corinthians 1:25). Socrates' death was noble, beautiful, and exalted, and it fitted in well with the ideals of Greek wisdom. But Glaucon in Plato's *Republic* proposes an ultimate test of the justice of the just man, which is more applicable to the case of Jesus than of Socrates. He says:

Let him be clothed in justice only, and have no other covering. . . . Let him be the best of men, and let him be thought the worst: then he will be put to the proof, and we shall see whether he will be affected by the fear of infamy and its consequences. . . . (And) the just man who is thought unjust will be scourged, racked, bound . . . and, at last, after suffering every kind of evil, he will be impaled.[11]

Glaucon's conditions for testing a just man were more than carried out in Jesus' suffering and dying. Moreover, Jesus' concern for others and for his Father, and the victorious way in which he died, completely outstrip the power and excellence of the Greek imagination in its search for an ideal test of justice.

But it is the redemptive character of the death of Jesus which most separates it from the deaths of Socrates and Buddha. Jesus was the historical realization of the Isaian "suffering servant," who "was pierced through for our faults, crushed for our sins" (Isaiah 53:5). Jesus, unlike Buddha or Socrates, took the whole weight of mankind's sinfulness on his shoulders and died for everyone; through his passion and death he gave all mankind an example of how to suffer and how to die. There is a healing meaning in this which is available to every person as he faces death.

In his dying, Jesus is a model and a gracious source of strength for all of us who must die sooner or later. By freely taking death upon himself, Jesus not only redeemed us from our sins but also gave us the power to conquer the effect of sin, death, by showing us how to die. He showed us that fear, anxiety, and apprehension in the face of suffering and dying are natural feelings, not to be ashamed of, because physical disintegration is an enemy of man's unity as inspirited flesh and is naturally repugnant. But he also showed us that if properly understood and participated in, physical disintegration can be the pathway to a higher mode of integration, that of resurrection. From this perspective, dying can be seen as a supreme form of positive disintegration, in which a person yields up his present state of integration in order to receive the gift of higher existence and self-transcendence.

Teilhard de Chardin has spoken of what I call the positive disintegration of dying in terms of growth and communion through diminishment. As long as man is living in this world, he is not yet totally transformed into the perfect Christ-self, and there is a need for a radical ex-centration. This reversion to God can only be accomplished through dying. As Teilhard so beautifully expressed it:

Now the great victory of the Creator and Redeemer, in the Christian vision, is to have transformed what is in itself a universal power of diminishment and extinction into an essentially life-giving factor. God must, in some way or other, make room for Himself, hollowing us out and emptying us, if He is finally to penetrate into us. And in order to assimilate us in Him, He must break down the molecules of our being so as to re-cast and re-model us. The function of death is to provide the necessary entrance into our innermost selves.[12]

By freely taking death upon himself, Jesus showed us that we, through him, can take death upon ourselves and be victorious in our dying, just as he was. By their sharing in the mind of Jesus, many saints are able to face death with "hilarity of spirit" and actual joy, as Thomas More did. Those who, through their participation in the Christ-consciousness, come to see death as it really is know that it is not annihilation but transformation, the pathway to a mode of existence that surpasses the wildest dreams of the heart in its excellence, beauty, and vitality.

This touches upon the mysterious "joy in suffering" that characterizes the lives of the followers of Christ. The letters of Paul and Peter and James all speak of being joyful in suffering, and this emphasis is rooted in the example and teaching of Jesus himself. In the account of John, Jesus is portrayed as looking forward to his passion with a kind of eagerness:

Do not let your hearts be troubled or afraid.
You heard me say:
I am going away, and shall return.
If you loved me you would have been glad to know that
   I am going to the Father.

John 14:27f.

Jesus is depicted in this passage as asking his disciples to rejoice because he is going to the Father, even though he will go through the valley of death. It should be stressed that the Master does not ask more of his servants than of himself. If he asked his disciples to rejoice because he was going to the Father through his passion and death, then he too must have rejoiced that his hour had come. His joy was not a trivial, sentimental kind of joy, but arose from full commitment in love and was compatible with intense suffering, even psychic pain. His was the deep-set joy of the dying soldier who hears the cries of victory and knows that the cause he loved and fought for has been won. It was the joy that a man knows when he lays down his life for his friend and knows that he has saved him. Above all, Jesus' joy was that of an obedient, loving son who has done everything his Father asked and knows he has his Father's blessing.

Jesus suffered intensely on the cross, and does not seem to have had any feeling of sensible consolation. But it is a complete misunderstanding of the crucifixion if we see Jesus as overwhelmed by his sufferings, rather than as the master of them. If Jesus' victory over suffering and death was only shown in the resurrection, and in no way in his passion and death, there would be grave cause for doubting the truth of the resurrection. But Jesus was clearly the victor in his suffering and dying, as well as in his resurrection, and it is because of this that his followers are told to rejoice and are empowered to be victors in Christ the victor, in their own suffering and death and in their own resurrection.

There is a startling emphasis on joy in the epistles. Paul describes the early Christians as "thought most miserable and yet always rejoicing" (2 Corinthians 6:10). Of himself Paul says, "I am so proud of you that in all our trouble I am filled with consolation and my joy is overflowing" (2 Corinthians 7:4). In the letter to the Philippians, which he wrote while he was in jail, Paul expresses joy and some fourteen times urges his readers to rejoice, as in this passage: "If my blood has to be shed as part of your own sacrifice and offering—which is your faith—I shall still be happy and rejoice with all of you, and you must be just as happy and rejoice with me" (Philippians 2:17-18). In the first epistle of Peter, the author speaks of the afflictions the Christians must undergo, yet in the same sentence says they are "already filled with a joy so glorious that it cannot be described" (1 Peter 1:8). James begins his letter by telling his readers that they should rejoice in their trials (James 1:2). In the Acts of the Apostles, it is said that after the disciples were beaten "they left the presence of the Sanhedrin glad to have had the honor of suffering humiliation for the sake of the name" (Acts 5:41). The lives of the early Christians seem to have been pervaded by an almost intoxicated joy in suffering for the Lord.

The ecstatic kind of joy in suffering felt by the followers of Jesus and described in the epistles and in Acts is only fully explicable in the light of the resurrection. Though we have noted a deep-set joy present in the passion and dying of Jesus, there was not the intoxicated joy in suffering that his followers manifested in the postresurrection and post-Pentecost period. Jesus had prayed that his disciples might come to taste deeply of a joy that no man could take from them, and had promised that his followers would do greater things than he did. Surely one of these greater things is the ecstatic joy in suffering so characteristic of early Christians, and of many Christian martyrs and saints ever since. Jesus' glory was already present seminally in the passion and death, but it was only in the resurrection that the Father's blessing of his Son's work was fully and magnificently demonstrated. It was only in the light of the resurrection, through the indwelling power of the Spirit of Christ, that the Christians were given this intoxicating joy in the face of suffering.

There is no contradiction or conflict between the emphasis on the good news of healing in this book and the mysterious Christian joy in suffering. This joy has nothing to do with a masochistic or sadistic inauthenticity, but in everything the enlightened Christian does and experiences he seeks to bring healing through the life-giving light of Christ, to wipe out as much as he can of the misery of the world. Where the Christian sees sadness he seeks to bring joy, through prayer and his own loving presence; where he sees illness in body or mind or spirit, in individuals or in society, he strives in every way possible to bring wholeness and fullness of life; where he sees anger, discord, hatred, strife, or war he seeks to be loving, to forgive, to be a peacemaker and a source of beneficence and benevolence.

Whatever Christian joy in suffering means, it does not mean apathy in the face of evil, or indifference to the agonies of mankind. It is never a sick delight in suffering for its own sake; it is never an excuse for inaction when confronted with individual or social evil. Rather, it is a joy that arises from the experience of victory over persecution and trials, the joy that a lover feels when he can show his love, even—perhaps above all—in very difficult circumstances. Christian joy in suffering is the joy that is born of victory and transcendence in every circumstance, even in sickness, persecution, imprisonment, beatings, and death. Paul expressed well the source of the joy of all victors in Christ the victor when he wrote:

Nothing, therefore, can come between us and the love of Christ, even if we are troubled or worried, or being persecuted, or lacking food or clothes or being threatened or even attacked. . . . *These are the trials through which we triumph.*

Romans 8:35-37, italics added

NOTES

1. Bernard Lonergan, *De Verbo Incarnato* (Rome: Gregorian Press, 1961), pp. 502–543.

2. William Ernest Henley, *Invictus*, lines 5–8.

3. Cited by Edward F. Edinger, *Ego and Archetype* (New York: G. P. Putnam's Sons, 1972), p. 101.

4. Kazimierz Dabrowski, *Mental Growth through Positive Disintegration* (London: Gryf Publications, 1970).

5. Lawrence Kohlberg, "Indoctrination versus Relativity in Value Education," *Zygon* 6 (1971): 285–310.

6. Columba Marmion, *Christ in His Mysteries* (St. Louis: B. Herder, 1923).

7. Elizabeth Kubler-Ross, *On Death and Dying* (New York: Macmillan Company, 1971).

8. Aelred Graham, *The End of Religion* (New York: Harcourt Brace Jovanovich, 1971), p. 164, footnote 47.

9. *Ibid.*, p. 53.

10. Edward J. Thomas, *The Life of Buddha* (London: Routledge and Kegan, 1960), p. 151.

11. Plato, *Republic*, trans. B. Jowett (New York: Random House), Book II, 361.

12. Teilhard de Chardin, *The Divine Milieu* (New York: Harper & Brothers, 1960), p. 61.

VI

Transcendence, Indwelling, and Service

THE HUMAN HEART hungers and thirsts for eternal life. Self-transcendence is both the royal road to, and in its higher modes a participation in, eternal life. Service on behalf of others is the richest and most eloquent sign that one is progressing along the pathway of self-transcendence and already possesses "a spring inside him welling up to eternal life" (John 4:14) and the indwelling Spirit of God.

Still, we must ask what this eternal life is which the human spirit is called to share in. John gives us the answer when he writes: "And eternal life is this: / to know you, / the only true God, / and Jesus Christ whom you have sent" (John 17:3).

The eternal life which the human heart yearns for is communion in knowledge and love with the Father, his Son Jesus and their Spirit, and with all others and the universe itself in God. Eternal life is the indwelling of lover in the beloved, of God in the enlightened individual, and of the enlightened one in God.

The expressions "transcendence," "indwelling," and "service" are intended to highlight the main themes of this final chapter in which I try to bring together key ideas present throughout the book and to explore yet more deeply the process of healing through enlightenment. The notion of *transcendence* points to the modes of actively receiving the gifts of healing through enlightenment. *Indwelling* expresses the dynamic inner state of being of the enlightened individual. *Service* heads the list of the fruits of enlightenment. Actually no rigorous separation of these three dynamic aspects of the healing through enlightenment process is possible or intended. Transcendence is for the sake of indwelling, and indwelling apart from its fruitfulness is meaningless.

Transcendence

The human person in his natural selfhood is a dynamic openness to transcendence. He is that being who only becomes himself in transcending himself, in moving from a state of potentiality to dynamic actuality. Man, for example, is made to know and love. But to know and love are acts of self-transcendence. Through knowledge, a person goes beyond himself into the world of being. Knowing is cognitive self-transcendence, as Bernard Lonergan puts it, and through it, the individual actually becomes more richly himself. Likewise, through loving, a person goes beyond himself and enters into communion with others. Love then is a certain ecstasy, a going beyond the self. But, paradoxically, it is only through the self-transcendence of love that a person really finds himself and realizes his true self. Again, the individual in his natural selfhood is oriented toward value, toward the worthwhile, and toward the truly good. Man, in other words, is naturally a moral being. But to act morally is to transcend one's self, to go beyond one's desires and fears, to overcome the pervading desire for personal satisfaction at all costs and the avoidance of pain in every instance, and to enter into the realm of the truly good and worthwhile. Moral self-transcendence, in other words, is a going beyond the apparent good to what is truly value-full and authentically worthwhile. Here once again, the paradox of self-transcendence is manifested. It is precisely by going beyond the confines of ego-centered satisfaction into the realm of true value that a person realizes his natural selfhood in its deepest moral orientations. Finally, the person in his natural selfhood is a desire for God. And through the gift of God's saving grace, he is given the power to satisfy the deepest yearnings of his heart, to receive the gift of the Christ-self, and to taste eternal life. The highest form of self-transcendence open to the human heart, then, is religious conversion. And this conversion, as we have seen, is a radical being-in-love with God in an unrestricted fashion. Through religious conversion, a person hands himself over to God in a total fashion, and in so doing, realizes his truest, richest, and deepest self. Man, accordingly, is that being who only becomes himself in actively receiving the gifts of ever deepening and enriching forms of self-transcendence.

In this chapter, I choose to speak of the healing-through-enlightenment process of self-transcendence as the ascending of a spiral of transcendence. The term "spiral" is used instead of "ladder" because the image of a spiral, as, for example, in a spiral staircase, includes the notion of covering the same points at ever higher levels. In healing through enlightenment, the human person is called to intensify at ever higher levels all the basic modes of self-transcendence. Thus, as a person is gradually transformed into the Christ-self through religious self-transcendence, he also continues to actualize the potentialities of the natural self through a self-transcending on the moral and cognitive levels. Religious, cognitive, and moral self-transcendence are not the only forms or modes of transcendence however.

Abraham Maslow lists some thirty-five forms of transcendence. And no doubt there are many more. Nevertheless, the most basic forms of self-transcendence seem to be the cognitive, moral, and religious, and all other forms are somehow involved with, and pervaded by, these three.

In what immediately follows, I wish to consider briefly some other important modes of transcendence which are involved in healing through enlightenment. Some pertain more directly to the area of the person's internal harmony with himself. Others relate to the individual's harmony with nature, with others, and with the works of his own hands. Finally, some concern directly the person's harmony with the Love-Intelligence that is God. At all times, however, these modes of transcendence are dynamically interrelated. And the increase of harmony in any one area at once effects a deepening harmony in all the other areas.

TRANSCENDENCE AND HARMONY WITH THE SELF

Man is that being who can fail to be in harmony with himself. As Christ warned the Pharisees, "Clean the inside of the cup and dish first, so that the outside may become clean as well" (Matthew 23:26). The metaphor of cleaning the cup and dish is used to urge the Pharisees to renounce their hypocrisy and to become as pure and wholesome within as they appear to be from without. Moreover, Christ's exhortation to the Pharisees is meant for all of us in varying degrees. But it is above all through the gift of a new heart in religious conversion that the human person comes into harmony with his true self. Yet, even the just fail often (Proverbs 24:16) and are subject in varying degrees to existential ignorance. There is consequently much need for constant vigilance, for existential diagnosis and mind-fasting, and for self-transcendence in its many forms.

Now, in ascending the spiral of transcendence toward

total harmony, four modes of self-transcendence take place which are closely related to existential diagnosis and which foster an ever richer harmony with the deepest aspirations of the self. More specifically, the practice of existential diagnosis and mind-fasting leads to the transcendence of (1) mind-body dualism, (2) pleasure-pain dualism, (3) cause-effect thinking, and (4) temporal servitude.

MIND-BODY DUALISM

Existential diagnosis is first of all a way of transcending mind-body dualism. Christotherapy views the human being as incarnate spirit, as a unity of matter and spirit. And existential diagnosis recognizes in body language a conscious or unconscious manifestation of mind and spirit. The trained therapist can uncover existential meaning in the movement of hands, the tone of voice, and the presence or absence of muscular tension. Through existential diagnosis, the individual is helped to transcend any tendency to divide himself into airtight compartments. He is enabled to understand and love himself as a unity. Existential diagnosis, accordingly, enables the individual to come into dynamic harmony with himself and to make the inside and outside one.

PLEASURE-PAIN DUALISM

Existential diagnosis enables one to transcend the pleasure-pain dualism. For many individuals, pain is identified with disease and pleasure with health. Accordingly, the quest for pleasure and the avoidance of pain tend to become the dominant theme in such an individual's life and thought-style. Existential diagnosis, on the other hand, reveals that it is not the pursuit of pleasure and flight from pain which lead to health and wholeness, but rather, the discovery of true meaning and value. Through existential diagnosis, one can transcend the futile and vicious cycle of the pleasure-pain dualism and become responsively open both to the healing meanings and to the calls to self-transcendence present in disharmony and disease.

CAUSE-EFFECT THINKING

Again, the reverent practice of existential diagnosis aids in moving beyond mere cause-effect thinking into the healing realm of true meaning and value. To grasp the precise nature of this self-transcendence, it would be helpful to contrast briefly Christotherapy with two leading schools of contemporary psychotherapy. The first views mental illness from a biophysical perspective. The psychiatrist who is radically biophysical in his approach will tend to seek the causes of mental illness in genetic and organic dysfunctions. He will recommend the use of drugs or of surgery as the best means of handling mental illness. The second reduces the causal basis of mental illness to childhood anxieties and to unconscious defenses developed to cope with them. The psychiatrist who is strictly psychoanalytic in his approach will view depth analysis of the past as the most effective means of bringing about psychic healing. Christotherapy, however, in close dependence on the existential psychotherapy of Thomas Hora, among others, places a primary emphasis on the present and tends to envisage mental "disease"—and, often enough, bodily "disease"—as a manifestation of a misdirected, ignorant mode of being-and-thinking-in-the-world. Enlightenment is the discovery of authentic meaning and value within a climate of love and becomes the primary mode of healing. In this way, the practice of existential diagnosis leads beyond the cause-effect thinking of bio-physical and intrapsychic approaches and enters into the realm of existential meaning and value.

It should be added that Christotherapy does not deny a certain validity and importance to the biophysical, intra-psychic, or even the behavioral approaches to psychopathology. A specific mental "illness" may well be biophysical in nature, and in such a case, should be handled accordingly. In like manner many, if not all, adult anxieties have roots in the past. Christotherapy, nevertheless, seeks to place more emphasis on existential diagnosis and discernment within the present than on depth analysis of the past. Indeed, the only way to total wholeness and holiness is through the practice of authentic mind-fasting and spirit-feasting.

TEMPORAL SERVITUDE

To be in harmony with oneself is to possess proper exis-tential attitudes toward time. One's attitudes toward the past and future can in large measure shape one's present, and hence existential diagnosis and mind-fasting are also crucial in this area. For many, the past becomes a form of enslavement, while the future acts as a thief that robs the present of its rich significance. Frequently, there is a fear that what is negative in the past will repeat itself in the future; such fear paralyzes one's endeavors to act within the present. The past becomes the anticipated future. But as Hora once remarked, "for the Christian, there is no past and the future is now." Indeed, the heart of the Good News of Jesus Christ is that in him the past with its failures and losses is overcome and the future glorification of man and world is already seminally present in the now of God's Kingdom.

The prophet Isaiah prophesied long before Jesus that "though your sins are like scarlet, they shall be as white as snow" (Isaiah 1:18). And Jesus instructed his disciples to let the dead bury their dead (Matthew 8:22) and to work with him in the present. To allow past failures, sins, and losses to weigh heavily on one's shoulders is a form of profound existential ignorance and inauthentic remembrance which makes transformative growth and development in the present impossible. This is that destructive "remaining with the dead" which a contemporary thinker has written of. Rather, we are called to freedom from bondage and servitude to the past, through repentance and the acceptance of the Good News, through the gift of a "new heart" and the transcendence of the past in all its negative dimensions. There is a profound forgiving of oneself that arises out of a loving understanding of Christ's forgiving power. The past ceases to be a millstone around one's neck through the aid of the healing truth of Jesus Christ.

In regard to the future, Jesus taught us to hope and work for the full realization of the Kingdom of God among men. Yet the present is also rich with blessings and it is in the present that one must work out his salvation. As Paul expressed it: "Now is the favourable time; this is the day of salvation" (2 Corinthians 6:2). Most certainly there is a valid and vitally important Christian expectation of a yet unrealized dimension of the Kingdom still to be revealed. But this hope must not be used as an excuse for inaction in the present or for an inauthentic anxiousness regarding the future. Jesus himself warned us not to become victims of an inauthentic type of concern for the future (Matthew 6:34).

To come into true harmony with himself, accordingly, an individual must not allow himself to be enslaved either by the past or by the future at the expense of the present. This type of transcendence of certain temporal servitudes is an aspect of the calling of every Christian and is in profound accord with certain contemporary psychotherapeutic insights. Thus, for example, a key emphasis in the psychological programs for recovering alcoholics is the need to adopt the proper mental attitudes toward the past, the present, and the future. The recovering alcoholic is taught never to let brooding over the past with all its failures cause him to despair and to give up in the present. He is likewise instructed never to let fear or excessive concern about what might transpire at some future date deter him from sobriety in the present. The slogan "24 hours at a time" is not some simplistic psychological gimmick; rather, it is an expression of deep wisdom and says something to every Christian regarding authentic attitudes toward the past, the present, and the future.

It is, of course, crucial to keep in mind that besides destructive mental attitudes toward the future there are also positive, authentic attitudes of mind and heart which are full of hope and enable the individual to work ardently for the realization of future goals and an ever fuller manifestation of the Kingdom of God on earth.

TRANSCENDENCE AND HARMONY WITH OTHERS

The human being is by nature social. He becomes his deepest self only by transcending the boundaries of the self and entering into communion with others. He must go out of himself in knowledge and love in order to find himself. Yet, according to the most fundamental law of human development, the only way one can truly become loving and understanding is by first being loved and understood by others. In the process of being loved and understood, one learns to love and understand both oneself and others. Through communion in knowledge and love, one overcomes the tendency to treat others as objects to be interpreted, analyzed, and dissected. Only then can a certain existential oneness of heart and mind be realized. The individual is thus called to transcend the subject-object dichotomy by entering into communion with others. Furthermore, though one initially needs the experience of being loved and understood in order to become loving and

understanding, once one is liberated from the solitary isolation of the ego, one then grows and develops to the extent
that he is loving and understanding toward others. As Hora
has written: "Communion is that union which makes dif-
ferentiation possible. Man becomes an individual through
participation. By losing himself in participation, he finds
himself as a 'presence.' "[1]

Man's goal, then, is to be a "presence" rather than an
"absence," to be self-transcending rather than self-
enclosing. In light of this, Martin Buber has appropriately
defined sin as a "remaining with oneself," whereas its oppo-
site is openness to others and ultimate responsiveness to the
Love-Intelligence that is God. The way to authentic existence in harmony with oneself, with others, and with transcendent mystery is through constant reverence, attentiveness, understanding, and love in the presence of others and
the Three who are the divine reality that is God.

Besides the subject-object dichotomy, there is what Hora
calls the motivational split of means and ends. Each of us
has the tendency to think exclusively in terms of self-
gratification and personal profit; and this leads us to vic-
timize people by using them for personal gratification and
enhancement. One who is ensnared by "means-end" thinking becomes unable to enter into authentic communion
with others, and this failure leads to constant misunderstanding and friction, to severe disturbance and dis-ease. On
the other hand, transcendence of "means-end" thinking
brings about the deep realization that each individual is an
image of God. Hence, every human being must be revered,
loved, and understood as a created sharer in the divine
likeness.

Finally, through the exercise of God's gift of self-
transcendence in authentic loving and understanding, one
slowly rises above the ties of family and race, nation and
culture, to enter into communion with all humanity. One

experiences kinship with all who have lived, are living, and will live in the future. For the Christian, there is the reality of the "communion of saints," so that even those who are dead still live. There is also the experience of profound communion with all those who are presently alive. The "Embrace, you millions" of Schiller's *Ode to Joy* becomes a felt desire and yearning. Finally, one experiences the deepest concern for those who are yet to live. This type of self-transcendence is not a misty-eyed romanticism but seeks to realize the goal of a unified humanity living in peace and dynamic harmony and hence a better world for those yet to be born. This transcendence of particularisms leads to healing through enlightenment on the social, cultural, and planetary levels, as well as in the realm of the I-Thou. Nor does this transcendence of particular bonds mean the denial or neglect of those values which lie in family, race, nation, or culture. Instead, all these bonds are preserved and encompassed within a universal love that extends to the entire community of man.

TRANSCENDENCE AND MAN'S HARMONY WITH NATURE AND TECHNOLOGY

The Christian sees nature as inseparably bound to man in the unfolding of his destiny. Nature, according to the Hebrew Testament, is God's cosmic word spoken to his children for their sake. "The heavens declare the glory of God, / the vault of heaven proclaims his handiwork" (Psalm 19:1). And in the New Testament, nature is depicted as bearing in itself the effects of man's sins, while yet yearning and groaning for its freedom from slavery and decay and for a share in the joyous glorification of the sons and daughters of God (Romans 8:18-23). This awareness of man's deep affinity with nature is reflected in the religious literature and poetry of East and West. In certain Eastern religions, man's kinship with nature is most strikingly expressed in profound reverence for life. In one of the West's most beloved of saints, Francis of Assisi, man's intimate bond with earth, moon, sun, and stars, together with all the living things of the universe, is celebrated in a most exquisite fashion in the *Canticle of Brother Sun.* In more recent times, the Romantic poets of England and the Transcendentalists of America were at times so intoxicated by the splendor and beauty of nature that they were led to speak of it as divine.

The acceleration of human cultural advances, however, and the rapid development of technology in recent times, has diminished man's sense of kinship with nature. But today, with the threat of ecological disaster, man is once again becoming acutely aware of his intimate bond with the natural forces around him. Man once again realizes that his destiny is inseparably bound to the air, earth, fire, and water which constitute his natural environment. Man came forth from the womb of Mother Earth, and he can survive only as long as she also remains alive and well and supportive. Contemporary man, then, is in need of cosmic self-transcendence through which he can bring cultural and technological achievements into a working harmony with the rhythms, elements, and forces of nature. Of course, nature is for the sake of man and man is called to subdue and transform the earth with both imagination and energy and to make it into an ever more suitable dwelling place for himself and his children. Yet, man is not absolute creator in the face of nature. It has dimensions and characteristics which must be respected. Man is thus called to reverence and respect and conserve as well as to transform and remold and utilize the elements of nature. Man must work out a balance between a hyperactivist technological spirit which would continue to erode farmland, contaminate water, wipe out forests, destroy animal life, pollute the air—all in the name of "progress"—and an excessive naturalism and conservationism which tries to halt abruptly technological advance and return man to an archaic, primitive state.

In a work on healing through enlightenment, it is essential to at least acknowledge man's abiding need for harmony between himself, the work of his own hands, and the elements and forces of nature. The aim of true enlightenment is holiness and wholeness. But, as long as man is alienated from his environment, he cannot be totally healed, blessed, and sanctified. Indeed, the ecological crisis which man faces today is a symptom of a profound interior malaise in the human heart. It is a call for existential diagnosis on a cosmic level. For just as bodily disease is a summons to self-transcendence, so also is ecological discord a call toward communal self-transcendence and existential diagnosis. It is a reminder that man is in deep need of that healing through enlightenment by which he can bring his own evolutionary development into harmony with the evolutionary exigencies and limitations of nature. In this respect, it is perhaps significant that the apocalyptic writings about the "end-times" speak of convulsions and changes in nature. For nature is, in a real sense, man's cosmic body. And thus, for man to contemplate nature is for him to read, as if reflected in a mirror, the interior features of his own heart and destiny.

TRANSCENDENCE AND HARMONY WITH LOVE-INTELLIGENCE

Man is that creature who experiences deep within himself the need to worship and adore. Carl Jung points out that the idea of an all-powerful divine being is rooted deep within the human psyche and that failure to acknowledge it will cause something else, usually something extremely inadequate and stupid, to be turned into a God. The point, from a Christian perspective, is that man is a being who must worship, and either he will worship and adore God or he will become an idolator in servitude to a false God.

The human person must choose between the worship of God and adoration of the self, between God-glorification and self-confirmation. To choose the latter is, in Hora's terms, to attempt to confirm the self as primary reality, to remain within the self, to be in an ever deepening state of alienation and aloneness, and to create a chasm between oneself and the rest of reality. To choose God-glorification, on the other hand, is to mount the spiral of transcendence, to be ecstatic in one's thinking, loving, and living, and to overcome all dualisms by entering into ever richer forms of communion and harmonious indwelling.

Making one's primary goal the gratification and confirmation of self dooms the self to loneliness and isolation. The human person is created to praise, reverence, and serve God and to love all else in God. By failing to acknowledge this basic drive and orientation, one radically frustrates the deepest longings of the self and sets oneself in diametric opposition to God and to all else that lives and moves and has its being in God. It is the idolatrous activity of man that lies at the root of all dualisms, whether body versus spirit, or self versus God and creation. Only by turning from idols toward the one, triune God can all dualisms be overcome.

God-glorification makes one more and more godlike, self-transcendent, ecstatic, and deeply at one with the self, others, creation, and God. Falling in love with the beauty and splendor and loveliness of God makes us all reflections of divine goodness. Man becomes like God when he comes to know and love as God knows and loves. Moreover, just as God shares what he loves with others through creation, so our falling in love with loveliness itself fills us with a desire to share our heart's delight with others. For God's creation is an act of divine self-transcendence which arises out of fullness, not out of a need to grow and become more perfect or to pass into some higher mode of being. God creates the universe, not to intensify his happiness or to acquire perfection but, rather, out of overflowing love for his own infinite richness and out of an ecstatic desire to manifest his glory to others and to let them share in his joy and plenitude. In like manner, man is called to be as God, to share in the inner splendor of divine life (2 Peter 1:4), and to draw others to this love of divine goodness and beauty, out of joy and a spirit of self-transcendence.

Another way to speak of this mode of transcendence is to note man's capacity for ecstasy. Basically, ecstasy is a matter of being lifted outside oneself, of standing outside oneself. There are, of course, many degrees and forms of ecstasy, but all point to the fact that the human person is called to be himself in moving beyond and outside himself. Indeed, man's capacity for ecstasy in its various forms is one of the richest signs that man is made for the beyond, for the yonder, for the mystery that is God. Whether it be the ecstasy of beholding a starlit night, the ecstasy of the mystic in the seventh heaven, or the ecstasy only lovers know—all are summons and pointers toward transcendence.

Ecstasy, it should be noted, is not the removal or destruction of ego or individuality but, rather, its deepest fulfillment. True enough, poets, mystics, and philosophers at times speak of ecstasy as if it meant the total loss of individuality. Thus, T. S. Eliot speaks of music heard so deeply that "you are the music while the music lasts,"[2] and Thomas Hora says that in the moment of insight or understanding there is no understander. Both point to an element in experience which is very real, but there is a certain hyperbole in their utterances. The individual in ecstasy is lifted out of his narrow concerns and interests, so that all his attention is riveted on the "other" of experience. Yet it remains the individual who is the subject of the experience, and consciously so. Indeed, the self is most perfectly and fully the self in the moment of peak experience and ecstasy. Once again, the paradox is realized that in the moment of the loss of the self in the other, the true self is found and actualized in a most perfect manner.

Indwelling

As all man's attempts at idolatrous confirmation of self as primary reality lead to dualism, polarization, and alienation, so every instance of authentic self-transcendence leads to at-one-ment, communion, harmony, and indwelling. Genesis depicts the overall effect of man's primal sin as expulsion from Paradise, where man once walked daily with God. The New Testament, on the other hand, expresses the effect of Christ's reconciling work as God dwelling within man's heart and man abiding in God. Hence, the chief effect of sin is isolation, while the principal work of grace is communion. Indwelling denotes the fullness of communion, for the deepest yearning of all lovers is to dwell within one another. And the Scriptures constantly speak of the indwelling of God in the spirit of man and of man's intimate abiding in God.

Actually, the Christian tradition speaks of two basic indwellings. The first is the indwelling of Father, Son, and Spirit within one.another. The second is the indwelling of Father, Son, and Spirit in the hearts of the righteous. Indeed, it is through the Father's gift of his Son and of their Spirit to mankind that we come to learn that deep within his heart, God is Triune. Here, of course, we are confronted with the richest truths of revelation. As the one God is Father, Son, and Spirit, a divine three dwelling within one another in infinite, loving ecstasy, so too are we called to share in this inner life of God, to dwell within the three just as they dwell within one another.

The mystery of man's participation in the interior life of God surpasses all understanding. John writes, "we are already the children of God, / but what we are to be in the future has not yet been revealed; / all we know is, that when it is revealed / we shall be like him / because we shall see him as he really is" (1 John 3:2). And Paul writes of "the things that no eye has seen and no ear has heard, things beyond the mind of man, all that God has prepared for those who love him" (1 Corinthians 2:9). What we do know, however, is what Jesus has revealed to us. The Father dwells in the Son and the Son in the Father, and together with their Spirit, even now, they come to set up their home in the hearts of all those who believe and accept the word of God. As Jesus put it, "If anyone loves me he will keep my word, / and my Father will love him, / and we shall come to him / and make our home with him" (John 14:23). And in like manner, Jesus promised to ask the Father to send us another Advocate to be with us forever, the Spirit of truth, if we but keep his commandments. The fruit of this indwelling will be, as he tells us: "you will understand that I am in my Father / and you in me and I in you" (John 14:20).

Clearly, God's indwelling in man is a mystery beyond all comprehension. Yet we must speak about it, since God has first spoken to us about it. Throughout the ages, the great writers and poets of the Christian Church have constantly attempted to utter the unutterable. Thus, the Fathers of the Church employed many metaphors to describe the dynamic intimate presence of the divine three to one another and to the hearts of the righteous. The Latins, for example, sedately spoke of the Father, Son, and Spirit as "sitting within one another." Certain of the Greek Fathers, however, according to their deeper mystical insight, preferred the terms of a dance. Thus, Father, Son, and Spirit dance within one another, and we are called to join in their divine dance of love. Perhaps the richest insight of all, however, is that we are called to be metamorphosed into images of the Son, so as to share in the inner life of God as sons and daughters in the Son. As the Son dances within Father and Spirit and calls them My Father and My Spirit, so shall we be able to call the Father and the Spirit ours as sons and daughters in the Son in a most true and loving fashion. Elizabeth of the Trinity loved to speak of the three who are the one God as "My Three," and in using this expression, she had perhaps a most profound insight into the richest meaning of the Good News of Revelation.

Entry into harmony with the three who are God means that the enlightened are also in harmony with all things in creation which are suffused with the love of God. As Jesus prayed to his Father in the last discourse recounted by John, "All I have is yours / and all you have is mine" (John 17:10), so God likewise speaks these words to all who truly love him. Hence, John of the Cross can write, "All the things of God and the soul are one in participant transformation. And the soul seems to be God rather than the soul, and is indeed God by participation."[3] Truly, the enlightened one who loves the Lord shall possess a hundredfold and indeed all creation, so that as Paul expresses it, "Paul, Apollos, Cephas, the world, life and death, the present and future, are all your servants; but you belong to Christ and Christ belongs to God" (1 Corinthians 3:22-23). Everything is at the service of God's enlightened ones, belonging to them, just as they in turn belong to Christ, and Christ to the Father. But the end will be when Christ himself turns over all things to the Father, and God will be all in all. "And when everything is subjected to him, then the Son himself will be subject in his turn to the One who subjected all things to him, so that God may be all in all" (1 Corinthians 15:28).

Service

The ascension of the spiral of transcendence is for the sake of indwelling. And the proof and sign of God's indwelling reality in one's heart is abundant fruitfulness and service. Christ stressed that the soundness of a tree lies in its fruitfulness (Matthew 7:17). And for Paul, the indwelling of the Holy Spirit necessarily manifests itself through the qualities of mind, spirit, and action which shine forth in the life of the enlightened individual. There is thus no better way to conclude this chapter and book than to reflect briefly on certain modes of being which the Spirit of God instills in the lives of God's holy ones. Clearly, "the stars differ from each other in brightness" (1 Corinthians 15:41), and those who are perfected in Christ are called to become yet more perfect (Philippians 3:12-16). Still, there are certain fruits which are present in the lives of all those who are indwelt and led by the Spirit of God. Among the fruits, Paul mentions "love, joy, peace, patience, kindness, goodness, trustfulness, gentleness and self-control" (Galatians 5:22-23). Of course, love, together with the service which flows from love, is the deepest expression of God's indwelling. But two basic spiritual qualities which exist within love's constellation are faith and hope.

FAITH

The enlightened one of God is characterized by profound faith. This faith is a created sharing in divine light, an inward gift of knowledge, the "eye of love," as Lonergan describes it, which enables one to apprehend, believe in, and respond to the highest of values. Through faith, the enlightened individual finds the universe friendly with a power, a wisdom, a love that broods at the heart of things and overcomes all evil. Through the gift of faith, the individual is enabled at once to share in the boundless, soaring confidence of the man of the 91st Psalm and in the trustful surrender of the man of sorrows so movingly portrayed in the book of Isaiah. Like the man of the 91st Psalm, the enlightened one of God has absolute confidence in God. He dwells in the shelter of the Most High. He is not afraid of any evils, whether they arise at noon day, in the morning, or in the midnight darkness. He is guided by a singular providence. The angels of God brood over him to see that he does not dash his foot against a stone. God will be with him in distress and will deliver him and glorify him. Like the man of sorrows, on the other hand, and like his master Jesus, the enlightened one does not flee from all suffering, but he passes through the crucible of suffering out of redemptive love for others, with a firm trust and confidence that the Father is with him in all his difficulties and will infallibly exalt him. And so it shall be for those who follow the Master. Hence, the enlightened ones of God trust that the Lord will guide them in all things and that in the end, as Julian of Norwich put it, "all things shall be well . . . and all manner of things shall be well."[4] The enlightened ones share in the faith of Thomas Aquinas, who wrote that "nothing will happen to them [those who truly trust God and serve him] that is not for their own good, and everything that happens to them will be to their own advantage."[5]

HOPE

In close conjunction with faith there is hope. The Hebrew Testament breathes an atmosphere of hope and expectation, even though there is no word there which corresponds exactly with the Christian notion of hope. God is the "hope of Israel" (Jeremiah 14:8). The prophet Jeremiah offers hope for a new covenant written on the hearts of the people, and Ezekiel clings to the promise that God will remember his covenant with Israel (Ezekiel 16:59ff). Isaiah also presents the hope of a restoration based on the covenant promises of God (Isaiah 55:3).

It is in the New Testament that the notion of hope reaches full blossom. Jesus, for example, gave the people grounds for a hope that was stronger than death when he argued for a future resurrection of the dead by saying that God is "God, not of the dead, but of the living" (Mark 12:27). Jesus pointed out that God said to Moses in the bush: "I am the God of Abraham, the God of Isaac and the God of Jacob" (Exodus 3:6). For Jesus this meant that God who revealed himself to the patriarchs and made covenants with them would not let them die forever but would raise them up to be with him. Of course, in the resurrection of Jesus from the dead the whole hope of the Christian resides. Paul in his writings indicates that the Christian is saved by hope (Romans 8:24), and hope is above all hope in the resurrection and the glorification that is to come. Hope also regards the realization of God's Kingdom on earth and it is communal, as well as individual, in its orientation and, in fact, embraces the whole of creation.

The enlightened individual believes that Christ is victorious and has confidence that he and his fellow believers and even the material universe are called to be victorious with Christ in his victory. There is, then, no room in the consciousness of the enlightened Christian for a despairing attitude either about his own salvation or that of others. In fact, the Christian in whom the Spirit dwells is called to hope vigorously for the salvation of others just as he does for his own salvation. Likewise, authentic Christian hope in no way leads to an unconcern for the healing of present evils and for the transformation of the earth through loving service. Rather, the enlightened Christian believes and hopes that by doing all he can in the present to heal, enlighten, and transform, he is even now building up the everlasting Body of the Lord and hastening the day of final glorification and the coming of a new heaven and a new earth.

LOVE

The foundation of faith and hope is love. As we have seen, God's self-transcending act of creation flows out of his ecstatic delighted love of his own divine goodness and a selfless desire to call others to share freely in the love of his goodness. The most fundamental form of love, then, is not *eros*, which is the seeking of good for oneself, nor *agape*, which is the seeking of the good for another. Love in its most radical form is an affirmative and affective assenting to and delighting in being, most especially personal being, because it is good, worthwhile and value-full in and of itself. The reason, then, why God loves his own being is because it is infinitely good, worthwhile, and lovable in itself. Likewise, the most radical form of human love is an affirmative, affective response to, and delighted repose in, the unique goodness, value, and loveliness of another human being.[6]

God's love for himself is born of knowledge of himself. The Father, in understanding the divine essence, generates his Word and breathes forth the Spirit of love. Similarly, human love is normally born of knowledge. But this is not always the case. When human beings fall in love, the love is disproportionate to and outstrips the knowledge. And, in the realm of God's love for man, there is God's gift of his love flooding our hearts through the Holy Spirit who is given to us (Romans 5:5). This gift of a sharing in the divine love precedes knowledge. Indeed, faith or the eye of love, which is our participation in this life in the light of God, is knowledge born of the gift of divine love.

Love is essential to enlightenment, and the process of self-transcendence in healing through enlightenment involves the vital intercommunion of knowledge and love in each of its stages. With this relationship between knowing and loving clearly in mind, we can now proceed to envisage the "man of loving enlightenment" in some of his spiritual qualities.

The enlightened loving individual is filled with the spirit of freedom. He participates in the very freedom of the children of God. He has no anxiety or fear. Christ urged his followers not to be anxious or worried (Matthew 6:25) and Francis de Sales noted that anxiety is the greatest evil that can befall a man, sin alone excepted.[7] Holy Scripture promises, however, that "in love there can be no fear, but fear is driven out by perfect love" (1 John 4:18). The healing power of love, then, is the key secret of all great religions, and it likewise lies at the heart of contemporary psychotherapies which place love at the center. Indeed, Thomas Hora has so verified the power of enlightened love to cast out fear and anxieties that he has written: "The experiential realization that there is no fear in love suffices for a complete commitment to a loving mode of being-in-the-world."[8]

Love, moreover, frees an individual to participate in the very freedom of God himself. Through the possession of a loving consciousness and an open response to reality, the individual comes to know the truth that sets him free. The enlightened man of love comes to grasp the paradoxical truth that the more one seeks to be independent of all else, including God, the less self-realized and free one can become. On the other hand, the more one seeks to enter into harmonious communion with others and God through authentic self-transcendence, the more individualized, self-actualized, and free one actually becomes. As Rahner writes, "The free man is the man at one with God. Only if he abandons himself to God does he receive himself back—his freedom is identified in love with the freedom of God."[9]

Further, the man of loving enlightenment transcends the

dichotomy of activity versus passivity, and enters into harmonious accord with what truly is. He realizes through God's gracious light that the loving mode of consciousness renounces all calculative and manipulative thinking and, instead, listens with active receptivity. To receive actively the gift of loving consciousness is to "pay attention" and to learn to listen. Authentic "paying attention" is an interesting and important activity, because it is related to mindfasting in the same way that learning to listen is related to spirit-feasting. As Hora points out, to pay attention means that a payment must be made. The payment demanded is renunciation of all inauthentic thoughts, cherished assumptions, favored images, and sensuous gratifications. Yet, by paying such a "mental and affective currency," one is freed for the active reception of loving consciousness. Dying to the self and losing one's inauthentic mind allows one to open the inner eye of the spirit to authentic healing meanings and values in life.

Again, the loving individual is a beneficent and beneficial presence in the world. Unfortunately, there are both negative and positive modes of being present in the world. Negative presence is a self-centered presence, leading to disharmony and disease. Negative presence can be obtrusive, seductive, snobbish, and overbearing. It is a caricature of authentic presence, creating ever greater chasms between the self and all others. Authentic presence, on the other hand, overcomes all dualisms and is a source of blessings and enlightenment for all who experience it. For Hora, authentic, positive presence is "being in love with being loving." It is not calculative nor a mere benevolent humanitarianism nor a do-gooder attitude. Rather, it is the light-filled spontaneity of one who experiences both the excellence and the fulfillment of being loving for love's own sake. For such an individual, to love is to be, and he has no other desire than to be a translucent medium of Love-

Intelligence and to let the light of love shine in the faces of all who encounter him.

To be a beneficial presence in the world is what is meant by Christian service. In creating and sustaining the works of his hands, God ministers to the needs of his creatures. Christ throughout his life mediated the love of the Father to all mankind, by being present to us as one who serves (Luke 22:27). In turn, the sign that the Spirit of the Father and his Christ dwells within us is our selfless love and service on behalf of our brothers and sisters, flowing out of God's love poured forth into our hearts. The entire Hebrew tradition may be summed up in the two great commandments to love the Lord our God with the totality of our being and to love our neighbor as ourselves (Matthew 22:37-40). But in the discourse at the Last Supper, recreated for us by John, Jesus gave us the new commandment to love each other with the same selfless love with which he loves us (John 15:11-12). Moreover, the epistles of Paul and John echo this commandment, so that John is able to give God the most beautiful name of *Agape*, that is, the selfless seeking of good for others. "God is love / and anyone who lives in love lives in God, / and God lives in him" (1 John 4:16). Clearly, it is the loving mode of being-in-the-world that constitutes the very meaning and being of Christian life, reaching toward ever higher levels of transcendence and fuller healing through enlightenment.

What is perhaps most striking about the loving mode of being-in-the-world is the manner in which it regards enemies and the means it employs to overcome evil. In the Hebrew Scriptures, as Christ points out, it was an eye for an eye and a tooth for a tooth (Matthew 5:38). Yet Christ teaches us to love our enemies, pray for those who perse- cute us, and to repay harm with goodness. We must never respond to evil through revenge or strive to inflict evil on our enemies. Rather, one responds to evil through doing

good and being loving. Paul did not look upon the Sermon
on the Mount as pious exaggeration and hyperbole. He took
seriously the teachings of Jesus, making it quite clear that a
Christian should yield his private rights and seek no ven-
geance (Romans 13:10; 1 Corinthians 6:1ff.; Romans 12:19).
Paul taught that the follower of Christ is never to repay
evil with evil but always to "conquer it with good" (Romans
12:21). Returning love for hate and good for evil heaps
red-hot coals on the head of the enemy, since love conquers
all. Selfless love is the core of enlightened Christian existence, and as Paul so eloquently expresses it in his praise of
Christian love:

Love is always patient and kind; it is never jealous; love is never
boastful or conceited; it is never rude or selfish; it does not take
offence, and is not resentful. Love takes no pleasure in other
people's sins but delights in the truth; it is always ready to excuse,
to trust, to hope, and to endure whatever comes. . . . In short,
there are three things that last: faith, hope and love; and the
greatest of these is love.

1 Corinthians 13:4-7,13

Finally, among the many forms of service that are born of
the loving mode-of-being-in-the-world, none is more important than the intercessory prayers of the holy and enlightened. Holy Scripture is full of exhortations to pray for
one another and the value of intercessory prayer is constantly affirmed. In Genesis, Abraham's pleading brings
forth God's promise to spare Sodom, even if there are only
ten just men in the whole city (Genesis 18). And James tells
us that "the heartfelt prayer of a good man works very
powerfully" (James 5:16). Of course, only if the Spirit
prays within us are our prayers infallibly heard. Yet God
works through his holy ones and he requires their prayers if
his work is to be accomplished. It was by no means an idle
remark when Jesus said to his disciples: "The harvest is rich
but the labourers are few, so ask the Lord of the harvest to

send labourers to his harvest" (Luke 10:2). The enlightened loving individual, then, is one who prays constantly for others and is rewarded for his perseverance. For this reason it is most important for those desiring healing through enlightenment to seek out the holy ones of God and to rejoice in the healing power of their prayers.

This book has been written for the consolation of those who are in desperate need of healing and as an encouragement for those healed and enlightened individuals who are dedicated to the task of bringing healing to others. A key element in the revelation of Jesus Christ is that in the divine healing process of redemption man must first receive before he can give. The gift of God's love poured forth by the Spirit of Christ must first flood a person's heart before he can become an effective instrument mediating the healing power of divine love to others. But of equal importance in the message of Jesus is the vital truth that once an individual has experienced the divine gifts of healing through enlightenment in himself he *must* go forth to share them with others. The light, once received, cannot be hidden but must be shared with others.

Clearly, contemporary man is in urgent need of healing in all areas of life. The individual with cancer needs healing and the underdeveloped nations of the world need healing. The individual neurotic and psychotic need the experience of a healing love, and whole societies enslaved by materialistic and ideological goals and ambitions need healing through enlightenment.

It might be asked what the relationship is between the therapy of enlightenment proposed in the present book and the important issues of emancipation, freedom, and world justice so pervasive in contemporary discussions. These latter concerns are found in the theologies of Edward Schillebeeckx and Johannes B. Metz, in the critical social theories of Herbert Marcuse and Jürgen Habermas, and in the liberation theologies of Third World Christians and others.

The primary focus of this book has been on the process of healing through enlightenment as it takes place in individual lives. Attention has been drawn, however, to the fact that the "gates of hell" have a social and collective dimension about them as well as an individual one. Also, I have suggested that much of the suffering—physical, psychological, and spiritual—of the individual is the result of environmental and social forces. In this line, Karl Menninger has recently said that the greatest sin of modern man is the indifference to what government does in the name of the citizen. Clearly, existential ignorance abounds not only on the individual level but also on the group and national and international levels as well. There is then a need for mind-fasting and spirit-feasting on the social as well as on the individual level. Another book, however, would be required to apply the principles of Christotherapy to the vital areas of social reform and international justice. Such a further application, however, is vital and necessary even for a completely effective application of the principles of Christotherapy on the more individual level. I hope to make such an application, perhaps on a collaborative basis, at a later date.

Happily, there are in existence today many Christian groups dedicated to the task of healing the ills of humanity and there is an ever growing sense of the need for religion to bring healing in all the dimensions of human existence if it is to prove a viable and vital force in the contemporary world. The aim of the present book has been simply to stress the need of the human heart for healing through enlightenment and the tremendous power for healing that is present in the Christ-meaning and the Christ-value.

One hopes that individual Christians and women and

men everywhere who in some way experience the healing power of the Christ-meaning and value will continue to seek as individuals to bring healing through enlightenment to everyone they encounter. Also, may groups of individuals who have experienced the healing power of Christ's love and truth join together in ever greater numbers to form therapeutic centers where they may bring healing through enlightenment on a societal as well as on an individual level. Let us pray, therefore, that the Lord of the harvest may send an abundance of laborers into the fields.

NOTES

1. Hora, *In Quest of Wholeness*, ed. Jan Linthorst (Garden Grove, Calif.: Christian Counseling Service, Inc., 1972), p. 186.

2. T. S. Eliot, *The Dry Salvages*, lines 210ff.

3. Quoted by Thomas Merton, *Zen and the Birds of Appetite* (New York: New Directions, 1968), pp. 119–120.

4. Quoted by F. C. Happold, *Mysticism* (Baltimore: Pelican Books, 1970), p. 330.

5. Thomas Aquinas, *De veritate*, q. 5. a. 7c.

6. Cf. Jules Toner, *The Experience of Love* (Washington, D.C.: Corpus Books, 1968).

7. Francis de Sales, *Introduction to the Devout Life*, IV, p. xi.

8. Thomas Hora, *In Quest of Wholeness*, p. 146.

9. Karl Rahner, "Freedom," *Sacramentum Mundi* (New York: Herder and Herder, 1968), II, p. 359.

Appendix

A. The Good News of Healing

THE HEALING HAPPENING that is Jesus Christ is too rich to be encapsulated in any simple formula. Jesus during his lifetime healed people who were suffering physically, psychically, and spiritually. Through his Spirit, Jesus continues to exercise that healing power in the churches and everywhere in the world in the hearts of women and men of good will.

To grasp concretely the meaning of Jesus' healing activity both for his contemporaries and for us today, it is vitally important to focus attention on the Hebrew Testament and its understanding of the relationship between sin and human suffering as well as its hopes for redemption. For Jesus was a Jew who grew up nurtured by the ancient beliefs, traditions, and cultural heritage of his people, and the Gospel writers portray Jesus as the Saviour of Israel and the one who came to fulfill the deepest yearnings of his people for redemption and the establishment of the Kingdom of God.

Human Sin and World Suffering

One of the key Hebrew Testament insights is the understanding of a radical connection between human sinfulness

164

and the existence in the world of sickness, suffering, and death. It is the primal sin of Adam and Eve that unleashes the forces of destruction in the world and there is no affliction or disaster in the personal or social life of Adam's posterity or in nature which does not have its radical ground in human sinfulness.

In Genesis 1-2:4 God is portrayed as creating all things, looking upon his work, blessing it, and seeing that "indeed it was very good" (Genesis 1:31). In Genesis 3, however, through the literary story of the "fall," the progenitors of the human race are depicted as introducing disharmony into God's good creation through an act of deliberate disobedience or sin. As a result of this willful flouting of God's command the good relations that existed between Yahweh and the beings created in his image and likeness are ruptured and the curse of alienation, suffering, and death falls upon the latter.

In the later chapters of Genesis and throughout the books of the Hebrew Testament the spread of the poison of sin and its effects is portrayed. As Genesis puts it: "The earth grew corrupt in God's sight, and filled with violence. God contemplated the earth: it was corrupt, for corrupt were the ways of all flesh on the earth" (Genesis 6:11). And even after the deluge man continues to sin and to experience the effects of sin which are violence, sickness, suffering of every type, and spiritual and physical death. In the words of the book of Wisdom:

God did make man imperishable,
he made him in the image of his own nature;
it was the devil's envy that brought death into the world,
as those who are his partners will discover.

Wisdom 2:23-24

A key point to grasp in regard to the Hebrew Testament understanding of sin and its effects is that it is in the human race, and not in God who is good, that sin has its origin.

The Hebrew Testament absolves God from all blame for sin and sees the evil of sin as arising from the human heart as it freely yields to the blandishments of the devil.

The Hebrew Testament speaks of sin in many ways. Sin is a "missing the mark," a failure to reach the goal. Sin is a deviation, a corruption of the person. Sin is a violation of a covenant; it is rebellion. Sin is guilt producing. Sin is folly and the sinner is a fool (Deuteronomy 32:6). Sin is a lie; it is deceitful and disordered. Sin means trouble and the sinner is a troublemaker not only for himself but for others. Sin is a refusal to know God, to accept and recognize his reality. Sin is a deliberate and willful act for which the person must bear full responsibility. Sin is in the individual but it has a communitarian dimension. The prophets interpret the fall of Israel as the necessary consequence of national guilt.

What the exact relationship is between sickness, suffering, and death on the one hand, and the sin of the human race on the other, has a long development in Hebrew thought. The belief in the afterlife came late in Judaic thought. Naturally enough, in the light of the Jewish belief in the justice of God, this meant a strong emphasis on the rewards and punishments in this life. In the Hebrew Testament, Yahweh is portrayed as the God who rewards the good and punishes the evil. Psalm 1 expresses the dominant Hebrew Testament view of God as rewarder of the just and punisher of the evil in this life:

Happy the man who follows not the counsel of the wicked . . .
But delights in the law of the Lord . . .
Whatever he does, prospers
Not so the wicked, not so;
they are like chaff which the wind drives away. . . .
For the Lord watches over the way of the just,
but the way of the wicked vanishes.

Psalm 1:1-4,6 (New American Bible)

Although the primary stress, especially in the earlier Hebrew Testament writings, is on Yahweh's immediate punishment of evil and rewarding of good conduct in this life, there is another view. Job, for example, is depicted in the most striking fashion as a just man who suffers. Job's friends tell him to examine his conscience to find out where he has offended Yahweh, and his wife despairingly tells him to curse God and die, but Job continues to protest his innocence. Finally, Yahweh vindicates Job, restores his losses and gives him double of all that he had before.

It is, however, above all in the suffering servant of Isaiah that the view that only the guilty suffer is shown to be radically inadequate. The Isaian Servant of Yahweh is portrayed as an innocent who bore in himself our diseases and sufferings so that through his wounds we might be healed (Isaiah 53). The Isaian servant suffers precisely because he is innocent and that enables him to bear the sufferings of others in a redemptive fashion.

The suffering servant of Isaiah represents one theme in Hebrew thought on sickness, suffering, and sin. It brings out a truth which Jesus will highlight later, above all in his own suffering and dying, namely, that an individual's sufferings are not necessarily the result of his own personal sins and can be redemptive in nature. It remains true, however, that the basic presence in the world of the evils of sickness, suffering, and death *as we experience them*[1] is due to the sinfulness of mankind.

Here it is perhaps appropriate to mention that Paul, who has the fullest theology of sin in the New Testament, builds upon and yet goes beyond the Genesis and Hebrew Testament's understandings of sin. In Romans 5:12-21 Paul argues from the universality of death in the world that all are "sinners" even though they have not sinned personally. Paul understands sin as a state or condition in which mankind exists. Paul does not mean that everyone personally commits the original or first sin of Adam. Rather, Paul holds that because all have a solidarity and unity with Adam because of their membership in the human race, they share in the condition which resulted from the sin of Adam. In Paul's view, then, all members of the human family are subject to death and the miseries of the human condition because of their sharing in a common bond with Adam. Finally, later Christian reflection will come to speak of "original sin" and its effects, which are concupiscence—the inability of the human being to concentrate wholeheartedly and singlemindedly on the pursuit of the good—and death, both spiritual and physical. These later reflections, of course, have their roots in both the Hebrew and the New Testament understandings of the relationship which exists between the original and personal sinfulness of mankind and the existence in the world of existential ignorance—an ignorance of authentic life values and meanings—and sickness, suffering, and death.

The Promise of Salvation

It is true that the Hebrew Testament picture of the human condition is at times quite discouraging. Man is portrayed as existing in a world burdened by greed, filled with the sufferings of the poor, the widowed, and the orphaned, permeated by ignorance, pain, and deprivation, and perverted by the wasteful and thoughtless lives of the rich and the powerful. Yet, although this picture of the world is bleak and somber and tends to evoke a sense of helplessness, still the Hebrew Testament does offer hope and indeed a most vital and dynamic hope. Thus, hidden behind the stark reality of sin and its devastating effects there was manifested from the beginning the gracious love of a God who still cared. The Hebrews learned that God was the one who would always be faithful despite man's own infidelities and abominations.

It is of course true that only when the fullness of time had come and God had sent his Son into the world (Galatians 4:4) could it be written that "however great the number of sins committed, grace was even greater" (Romans 5:20). Yet this does not mean that in a profound sense God's saving and healing intention was not also manifested from the beginning in his dealings with his sinful children. Thus, for example, immediately after the fall when God saw Adam cowering in the shame of his nakedness and sin he "made clothes out of skins for the man and his wife" (Genesis 3:21). Most importantly, however, against the serpent of the temptation God promised ultimate victory to the sons and daughters of Adam (Genesis 3:14-15). And it is God's promise of the final crushing of the offspring of the serpent which has come to be known as the "proto-evangelium," for it is the first announcing of the good news of victory over sin. It instilled hope in human hearts and showed that God's saving and healing activity was at work in the world from the moment of Adam and Eve's act of disobedience.

Throughout the Hebrew Testament period God continued to be present to mankind. Thus, the Lord called Abraham out of the land of Ur and promised Canaan to his descendants, and the promise was kept. Yahweh constantly renewed his covenant with his people, the Israelites, in spite of their infidelities. This was the faithfulness of God and the salvation that he brought to his people: victory, deliverance, the self-determination of the Hebrew peoples. Indeed, victory was an initial meaning of "salvation."

In the great Song of Moses that celebrated the Lord's victory over the Egyptians at the Sea of Reeds, Yahweh is glorified as the Lord who saves his people from the enemy and as the majestic healer of his chosen ones. He it is who in his steadfast love delivers his people from the onslaught of

their enemies as well as from all their diseases and affliction.

If you listen carefully to the voice of Yahweh your God and do
what is right in his eyes, if you pay attention to his commandments and keep his statutes, I shall inflict on you none of the evils
that I inflicted on the Egyptians, for it is I, Yahweh, who give
you healing.

Exodus 15:26

Clearly, in the great Exodus-event the ideas of God as
saviour and as healer are intimately associated. This is of
particular importance in view of the unique significance
and role of the Exodus-event in the unfolding of the history
of salvation.

There is a continuous deepening in the understanding of
the idea of salvation as the Hebrew Testament period advances. In the Psalms, God is begged for salvation from
enemies, from the wicked, from illnesses, and from every
form of distress. Especially with the postexilic period, the
notion of salvation becomes messianic in character. Salvation comes to be looked upon as freedom from all types of
evil, personal as well as collective, implying an ultimate
acquirement of complete and total security from all harm.
Finally, salvation becomes crystallized in the figure of the
Messiah to be sent by God to bring redemption to his people and to establish the reign of God upon earth.

Jesus Christ, the Healing Light

In the Event of Jesus Christ the conqueror of the seed of
the serpent and the long-awaited Saviour of Israel becomes
present to mankind. Luke, the physician-evangelist, in his
Gospel of joy recounts that on the night of Jesus' birth
angels appeared to shepherds announcing that a Saviour

had been born and that his advent meant peace for all who enjoy God's favor. Later when Jesus was presented in the Temple of Jerusalem the aged Simeon voiced on the part of the "poor of Israel" the recognition of Jesus as the promised Saviour and healer through enlightenment when he exclaimed in his Song:

Now, Master, you can let your servant go in peace,
just as you promised;
because my eyes have seen the salvation
which you have prepared for all the nations to see,
a light to enlighten the pagans
and the glory of your people Israel.

Luke 2:29-32 (italics added)

Jesus from the start is acknowledged as Saviour and healer of the whole person. In the New Testament the same Greek word *sōzein* is used to signify both saving and healing or making whole. Indeed, in the synoptic Gospels Jesus' saving activity is depicted as a healing but the word *sōzein* is used in a pregnant fashion to suggest that the healing is a sign or symbol of the conferral of a far greater salvation than just the health of the body. Actually, the body-soul distinction as we know it in the West is not a Hebrew, but basically a Greek, conception. Jesus, like his fellow Semites, viewed the human person as a unity and so to save and heal was to save and heal the whole person.

Certain key points should be kept in mind from the start if the truly *Good* News of the Gospels is to be deeply savored and understood. First, Jesus is by his very nature, presence, and mission the healer par excellence. Second, Jesus is healer of the whole person and frees him from all the effects of sin. Third, Jesus is light and heals through his light. Fourth, Jesus crowns all the healing efforts of his lifetime through the great healing events of his suffering, dying, rising, ascending into heaven, and sending of the Spirit.

Jesus the Healer

Jesus is by nature *the* healer because he is the incarnation of the salvation of God. If, as the King James Version expresses it, Yahweh may be described as "the health of my countenance and my God" (Psalm 42:11), Jesus may most properly be spoken of as the incarnate manifestation of the health and salvation of the Lord. Jesus, accordingly, did not heal simply to prove that he was from God or to show that he was compassionate or to give evidence of power but, most profoundly, simply because he was and forever is the very healing power of God made flesh. In Jesus "the kindness and love of God our saviour" (Titus 3:4) is manifested to all, and everyone who reaches out to him experiences the beneficent effects of his saving presence and power in every dimension of his being. Jesus himself then is the Good News, and the Good News is that Jesus saves us from our sins and heals us from all our afflictions.

To emphasize, however, that it was above all because of who he was and forever is that Jesus healed is not to deny that his healings were signs of the presence of the Kingdom of God among his people and a pledge and promise of greater healings and salvation yet to come. There was a tension in Jesus' teaching which expressed itself in an "already" and a "not yet." Jesus announced that the Kingdom of God was at hand and yet he also exhorted his disciples to pray that the Kingdom of God might come. Jesus' healings accordingly were both signs of the presence of the saving God among his people and a promise of a total and complete salvation that was yet to come.

Jesus, Healer of the Whole Person

Jesus came not only to make human persons spiritually whole and free from sin but also to make them physically and psychically integral as well. As already noted, the Semite viewed the person as a unity. Jesus, owing to his Semitic outlook but most profoundly to his divine sonship and the healing intention and intuitive mental excellence which he possessed, always dealt with the whole person. Jesus possessed a very intimate knowledge of the hearts of human individuals, and this helped him to deal with each one according to his deepest needs. As John wrote of Jesus: "He never needed evidence about any man; he could tell what a man had in him" (John 2:25).

The key importance of Jesus' role as healer of all the diseases of mankind is brought out in a variety of ways in the Gospels. There is, for example, the case where John the Baptist in prison and in a certain dark night of the spirit, sent his disciples to inquire of Jesus, "Are you the one who is to come or have we to wait for someone else?" (Luke 7:20). Jesus replied to John's anxious query:

> Go back and tell John what you have seen and heard: the blind see again, the lame walk, lepers are cleansed, and the deaf hear, the dead are raised to life, the Good News is proclaimed to the poor.
>
> Luke 7:22

Jesus here points to his healings and announcing of the Good News to the poor as *the* signs that he is "the one who is to come." Again, there is the instance Matthew recounts in the context of the Suffering Servant of Isaiah:

> That evening they brought him many who were possessed by devils. He cast out the spirits with a word and cured all who were sick. This was to fulfill the prophecy of Isaiah: *He took our sicknesses away and carried our diseases for us.*
>
> Matthew 8:16-17 *(italics added)*

In Matthew's eyes Jesus in his atonement ministry dealt with diseases and sicknesses of every type as well as with human sinfulness and ignorance. Hence, the Lord's healing work extends to the whole person, to body, mind, and psyche as well as spirit.

There is, moreover, no evidence that Jesus ever refused to heal an individual when this gift was sought with true faith. In fact, on one occasion when a leper seemed to suggest the possibility that it might not be Jesus' will to heal him by saying to him, "Sir . . . if you want to, you can cure me," Jesus replied almost with a touch of impatience, "Of course, I want to! Be cured" (Luke 5:12-13). The man was instantly cured. Jesus, it is true, did not go out of his way to seek out all who were sick in order to heal them of their spiritual, mental, and physical diseases. His brief ministry was limited to a narrow region of the Near East, and much of his time was spent either in the instruction of his disciples or in silent communion with the Father in prayer. Scripture clearly reveals, however, that Jesus did cure all those who came to him and reached out to him in confident faith. Jesus' healing power was blocked in its effectiveness only by lack of faith or by perversion of motive on the part of those who were looking for wonders or a magician's tricks.

Jesus, Healer through His Light

A further vital dimension of Jesus' healing ministry, an element most crucial for this work, is that Jesus was, is, and forever will be light, and that he healed and continues to heal through his being as light.

Yahweh is spoken of as light in the Hebrew Testament, and John in his Gospel describes Jesus as "the true light that enlightens all men" (John 1:9). To all who open themselves to his light Jesus gives the power to overcome the darkness and to become children of the light, children of God. Jesus then is the very light of God made flesh; and as he went about his earthly ministry being good and doing good and letting his light shine in the faces and hearts of men and women, faith and trust in him were born in human hearts—and the result was healing.

In the Gospel accounts the most frequent way in which healings take place is through faith in Jesus. Faith is the central form of enlightenment and it is at once an inward gift of the Father and a trust inspired by the light shining forth in the face of Jesus. The notion of healing through enlightenment accordingly perhaps expresses best what radically took place as Jesus went about his saving, healing ministry.

Again and again Jesus reveals to individuals that faith is a source of healing for them. To the woman afflicted with a hemorrhage, Jesus says: "My daughter, . . . your faith has restored you to health; go in peace and be free from your complaint" (Mark 5:34). To a man cleansed of leprosy Jesus says: "Stand up and go on your way. Your faith has saved you" (Luke 17:19). It is clearly faith in Jesus which is the most common factor operative in the various incidents of healing recorded in the Gospels. Jesus constantly demands faith, praises its presence, and indicates that unbelief renders his healing power ineffective.

And what, in the Gospels, is faith? In its most simple terms faith is an acceptance of Jesus in his person and in his message. It is an inward gift of God, a type of enlightenment, which enables the individual to trust in Jesus and to rely on him as one who is faithful and true.

The stress on the key role of faith in the healing process should not lead us to overlook the richly diverse ways in which Jesus led various individuals to wholeness and well-being. Jesus was in no way a simpleminded faith-healer who displayed more ignorance than insight or who demanded a univocal blind-faith response from everyone he met. Jesus was utterly unique and he dealt with each person according to his or her individual needs and character.

In what immediately follows I would like to look at certain incidents of healing which are described in the Gospels and to analyze them especially in the light of certain contemporary psychological insights. I realize that Jesus was not a psychologist in the modern sense, but I believe that he was acutely aware of the subtleties of human motivation and that such teachings as those of the Sermon on the Mount surpass, in their insight into the fears and desires of the human heart, many of the grounding insights of various contemporary psychotherapies. I should add at once that the Gospel accounts of Jesus' healings do not necessarily intend to be historically accurate in all their details. I do presuppose, however, that the Gospel accounts faithfully reflect certain key features and characteristics of the historical Jesus and his manner of healing. Finally, my own reflections are creatively interpretative in nature and should be understood as such.

In an incident described in John (John 5:1-8), Jesus met a sick man at the Pool of Bethzatha who had been waiting at the pool for a very long time in the hope of being cured. Strangely enough, Jesus asks him, "Do you want to be well again?" This question perhaps reflects an understanding on Jesus' part that this man still had to come to grips with himself in a vital way and to decide whether he really wanted to be cured or not. Frequently enough, individuals who give the appearance of wanting to be cured are in fact quite reluctant to give up the "security" of their diseases and to come to terms with reality without making use of defense mechanisms. Jesus accordingly required that the man at the pool acknowledge in his heart that he truly sought to be healed and made whole. When this had been done, Jesus cured him. Sometime later, Jesus again met the man and, with a warning which all men should heed, told him not to sin any more lest something worse should befall him. This is an instance where there is perhaps an implied relationship between personal sin and suffering. One should take note here of the various stages of enlightenment and healing through which Jesus led the man. First, Jesus brought the man to a self-confrontation so that a certain self-knowledge could emerge. Later, he made a special effort to lead him to a deeper understanding of his need for conversion in order to avoid catastrophes worse than his former illness.

Again, the ways that Jesus is reported to have dealt with the woman at the well in Samaria and with Bartimaeus, the blind man, serve to highlight the unique fashion in which Jesus handled individuals. To the woman at the well (John 4:5-42) Jesus revealed her past and in this way healed her by gradually leading her to a knowledge of the truth. To the pleas of Bartimaeus, the blind beggar, Jesus countered, "What do you wish me to do for you?" (Mark 10:51). It appears that perhaps what Bartimaeus deeply desired was not at all clear even to himself, and what he needed was to see more clearly what he really desired. Once Bartimaeus asked specifically for the gift of sight, Jesus gave it to him saying, "Go, your faith has saved you." Significantly, Bartimaeus immediately got up and followed Jesus along the road he was traveling. He had found more than mere physical sight. He had found the true light that enlightens every man.

The subtlety of Jesus' way of bringing healing through enlightenment is especially in evidence in the case of the healing of the Gerasene demoniac. This incident is remarkable for a number of its elements. Jesus had just calmed the storm at sea and this action is symbolic of the peace that Jesus brings to the human heart, as well as the healing of the rupture that sin caused between mankind and nature.

As soon as Jesus leaves the boat a crazed man—we might call him psychotic today—rushes up to him howling and shouting. This man

lived in the tombs and no one could secure him any more, even with a chain; because he had often been secured with fetters and chains but had snapped the chains and broken the fetters, and no one had the strength to control him. All night and all day, among the tombs and in the mountains, he would howl and gash himself with stones.

Mark 5:3-5

It is likely that this turn in events terrified the disciples greatly, since they had just escaped drowning and were now confronted with a possessed, insane man near a cemetery in the pitch dark of night. But what is perhaps most striking is that Jesus does not heal the man all at once. The man is described by Mark as being possessed by unclean spirits, and psychologically the man seems twisted and torn in many directions, divided and shattered in mind. Jesus attempts to drive out the unclean spirits, using the words: "Come out of the man, unclean spirit." When the spirit would not leave, Jesus asks for its name, for knowledge of a name was, for the Hebrews, synonymous with possessing power over that person. Once the name was uttered, the man was freed from the spirits, and his madness left him. As we see, Jesus through his exorcism brought this man to self-knowledge and hence to self-possession and healing. It is important to note that Jesus remained with the man for some time—perhaps all night—since Mark recounts that people from the nearby town came out to see what had happened, and there they found the demoniac who was now clothed and in full control of his senses. The transformation was total and it frightened the people. The naked, howling, self-wounding demoniac was now fully clothed, perfectly sane. Here is a most powerful example of the subtle manner in which Jesus often gradually led individuals in desperate need of wholeness through various stages of enlightenment until full healing occurred.

What appears, I believe, from the composite picture in the Gospel accounts of Jesus in action as healer is that he truly did know what was in individual human hearts and acted accordingly. Where Jesus saw unchasteness he gave purity of mind and heart. Where Jesus found disunity and fragmentation of spirit he restored integrity. Where Jesus saw physical and spiritual immobility he gave freedom of spirit and physical agility. In each instance Jesus knew what the real problem was, and through probing questions or strong commands or at times a gentle word of loving concern brought healing through his light.

Jesus, Healer through His Death and Resurrection

As we have seen, Jesus is portrayed in the Gospels as one who during his public ministry constantly sought to overcome the reign of sin in the world through the establishment of the Kingdom of God. Jesus, in fact, was referred to as a friend of sinners. Jesus did not befriend sinners because he condoned sin but, on the contrary, because it was sinners who were most in need of his help. Through his preaching the Good News, through his exorcisms and his healings, through his denunciations of every type of evil, Jesus opposed the reign of sin in the world and set himself on a collision course with the powers of darkness. It was accordingly in his suffering, dying, and rising that Jesus once and for all crushed the head of the seed of the serpent and won salvation for all who would accept it by believing in his name.

I would like to note here, in lapidary fashion, the way John the evangelist and Paul the apostle envisaged the suffering, dying, and rising of Jesus.

In the Gospel of John, Jesus is revealed as the Word made flesh, as the healing light of God which shines brightly in a world plunged in darkness. In everything Jesus says and does he opposes the reign of sin in the world. But it is above all in the hour of his passion that Jesus' victory over the powers of darkness is manifested. Indeed, John portrays the passion of Jesus as the beginning of his glorification. For Jesus prays at the Last Supper in what is known as his priestly prayer: "Father, the hour has come: / glorify your Son / so that your Son may glorify you" (John 17:1). And the Father does glorify the Son by strengthening him in his suffering and dying and, above all, by raising him from the dead. Most certainly Jesus was and is for John "a light that shines in the dark, / a light that darkness could not overpower" (John 1:5).

As for John, so also for Paul the passion, death, and resurrection of Jesus are the climactic saving events and the definitive overpowering in principle of the reign of sin in this world. Since for Paul death is the effect of sin, it is through the obedient death of Jesus Christ that sin is overcome. Thus, just as all died in Adam, so all are called to be alive in Christ. The follower of Christ is called to share in the death of Christ so that by dying to sin he may arise with Christ to a newness of life. In Paul more than in any other New Testament writer, Jesus appears as the conqueror of sin.

Most assuredly, Paul in the epistle to the Romans paints a very bleak and stark picture of man apart from God. Yet Paul's main point in stressing the wretchedness of sinful man apart from grace is simply to highlight through contrast the glorious state of those who share in the victorious grace of the risen Christ. Thus, where the sin of Adam affected man for the worse in body and spirit and even nature as well, Christ the new Adam, through his redeeming, transformative power, touches the whole man and nature as well for the better. Likewise, where sin deprived man of justice and holiness, Christ won the gift of the indwelling Spirit for man. And where sin plunged man into the darkness and slavery of ignorance, the truth that sets man free was made manifest in Christ. As Paul expresses it so exultantly: "If it is certain that through one man's fall so many died, it is even more certain that divine grace, coming through the one man, Jesus Christ, came to so many as an abundant free gift. . . . [And] if it is certain that death reigned over everyone as the consequence of one man's fall, it is even more certain that one man, Jesus Christ, will cause everyone to reign in life who receives the free gift that he does not deserve, of being made righteous" (Romans 5:15, 17).

B. Healing Signs in the Church

AFTER JESUS INAUGURATED his ministry of healing and preaching the Good News of the Kingdom, he appointed disciples to participate with him in his mission. When he sent out his chosen twelve, he gave them power to expel unclean spirits and to heal diseases of every kind (Matthew 10:1-8). When he appointed another seventy-two to go out on a mission, he instructed them to cure the sick and to say to the people that "the kingdom of God is very near to you" (Luke 10:9). Jesus commissioned his apostles and disciples to do as he himself did, performing those signs which were proof to John the Baptist that Jesus was indeed the "expected one." Moreover, just as it was one and the same thing for Jesus to announce the Good News of the Kingdom and to heal individuals of their afflictions, so was it to be for his disciples.

As the earthly ministry of Jesus drew to a close with his suffering, death, and resurrection, Jesus, according to the ending of Mark's Gospel, appeared to his chosen eleven for the last time and commanded them to "go out to the whole world" and to "proclaim the Good News to all creation" (Mark 16:16). Jesus promised that signs would accompany the believers, and that among the significant signs would be the following: "They will lay their hands on the sick, who will recover" (Mark 16:18).

The Acts of the Apostles marks the beginning of the time when Jesus is present through his Spirit to the Christian community. And in the Acts of the Apostles the vital connection between the proclamation of the Good News of the Kingdom, realized in Jesus, and healing is constantly in evidence. Wherever the Good News is preached, there the ministry of healing also takes place.

One of Peter's first acts after Pentecost was to heal a man crippled since birth, and so many miracles of healing took place through the hands of the apostles

that the sick were even taken out into the streets and laid on beds and sleeping mats in the hope that at least the shadow of Peter might fall across some of them as he went past. People even came crowding in from the towns around about Jerusalem, bringing with them their sick and those tormented by unclean spirits, and all of them were cured.

Acts 5:15-16

But Peter was quick to protest on behalf of the apostles that it was not due to some power or holiness of their own, but rather it was due to the name of Jesus and trust in his name that sick people were made whole. The healings performed by the apostles and disciples always took place within a context of faith and were signs of the healing presence of God in Jesus. Scripture tells us that it was the power of Jesus and faith in him that enabled Peter and John to be God's instruments in the healing of the crippled man: "It is the name of Jesus which, through our faith in it, has brought back the strength of this man whom you see here and who is well known" (Acts 3:16). In turn, the healed cripple was led to a new level of spiritual existence through the healing process, for "he went with them [Peter and

John] into the Temple, walking and jumping and praising
God" (Acts 3:8). A similar chain of events took place when,
as Acts recounts in a later chapter, Paul was able to be an
instrument of healing for a crippled man due to the latter's
faith in the power of Jesus: "Seeing that the man had the
faith to be cured, Paul said in a loud voice, 'Get to your
feet—stand up', and the cripple jumped up and began to
walk" (Acts 14:9f.). In both of the cures just mentioned faith
in the healing power of Jesus was a key element.

The Gift of Healing

The unity between the preaching of the Good News of
Jesus Christ and healing was a great and powerful sign that
the Kingdom of God was inaugurated on earth. This was
not, however, the only sign of the Lord's saving presence.
In the early Christian communities there were manifested
those signs which were called charisms or gifts and those
which from ancient times have been referred to as sacraments. The "gifts" were granted to various individuals in
the Christian community for the building up and
strengthening of the Church. The sacraments, on the other
hand, were those concrete manifestations and effective
signs of Christ's vital presence through his Spirit in the
Church, which were expressed in symbols and/or words
and administered in the Church. The gifts were freely
given by the Lord to various individuals within the Christian communities. The sacraments were the permanent possession of the Church and were effective signs of Christ's
constant presence to his holy people.

Among the many gifts which appeared in the early
Christian communities, Paul mentions the gift of healing.
Together with the other gifts, this charism of healing was
granted to specific individuals for the comforting and
strengthening of the People of God.

There is a variety of gifts but always the same Spirit; there are all sorts of service to be done, but always the same Lord. . . . One may have the gift of preaching with wisdom given him by the Spirit; another may have the gift of preaching instruction given him by the same Spirit; and another the gift of faith given by the same Spirit; another again the gift of healing, through this one Spirit.

1 Corinthians 12:4-9

The presence of various forms of healing within the Church did not cease with the death of the apostles, for the ancient Christian writers contined to speak of occurrences of healing and of Christians in their midst who were endowed by the Spirit with certain gifts. Irenaeus, for example, wrote about the frequency of cures brought about through the invocation of the name of Jesus and he spoke of some who uttered prophetic expressions and others who healed the sick by laying their hands upon them.[1] And Origen testified that Christians in his time received the gift of healing through which individuals were freed from madness and diseases of every type.[2]

The early years of the Church, which saw both the healing and preaching ministry of the original apostles and disciples and then the doctrinal controversies and spiritual writings of various Church Fathers, came to a close with the decline and disintegration of the Roman Empire. Augustine is a witness to this closing, and yet amid those dark days of Western civilization, Augustine explicitly witnesses to the continuing presence of healings in the Church.

In his great *City of God*, Augustine describes various miracles, including those of healing, which he personally witnessed. Augustine explicitly speaks of miracles of healing which were effected through the name of Christ and faith in his name. Augustine does not here refer to the charism of healing described by Paul in Corinthians, but he does indicate the presence in the Church of a nonsacramental mode of healing. This type of healing takes place through prayer to Christ in the context of martyrs and their relics. It is important to take note of this mode of healing because of its charismlike quality and its constant recurrence in subsequent ages of the Christian Church.

The veneration of martyrs was an early phenomenon in the Church and the custom of invoking their aid seems to have been a quite spontaneous and Spirit-inspired development. The early Christians saw in the martyrs victors in Christ-the-victor and sharers in the holiness, light, and healing power of Jesus. When Jesus walked the roads of Palestine it was enough at times, so the Gospel relates, to reach out and touch the hem of his garment with a God-inspired faith in order to be healed. After Jesus' death and resurrection, the Acts of the Apostles recounts that women and men of faith had only to let the shadow of Peter fall upon them in order to experience the healing power of Christ working in them. It was a natural enough development then, in later centuries, when Christians sought to come in contact with the healing power of Christ through the instrumentality of his martyrs and the relics connected with their victorious witnessing to the Lord.

Further, it was not, at least among enlightened Christians such as Augustine, a superstitious belief in the power of relics in themselves, nor even in the power of martyrs in themselves, that led them to acknowledge Christ's healing presence in his martyrs and saints. Augustine himself witnessed miracles of healing wrought through the martyr Stephen, but he made it clear that it was Christ who did the healing and that it was because Stephen laid down his life for his faith that Christ used him as an instrument of his healing.[3]

After the fall of Rome and throughout the centuries up to the present time, healings have continued to take place in the Christian churches through the instrumentality of martyrs and saints.

In the churches of Eastern Orthodoxy and in various Reformation churches, the bestowal of the gift of healing has been in evidence. According to certain historical accounts, Martin Luther, George Fox, and John Wesley, to name but three, proved effective instruments of healing for various individuals. And in Eastern Christian churches, instances of the charism of healing abound.

Interestingly, the Roman Catholic Church has almost without exception required the occurrence of miracles as a prerequisite for the beatification and canonization of saints. Generally, these miracles have been healings, and the Church's requirement that such miracles of healing take place flows perhaps most profoundly from the insight that to be a saint and to be an instrument of healing are one and the same thing. In this context, one need only think of such individuals as Martin of Tours, Gertrude the Great, Catherine of Siena, Vincent Ferrer, John Vianney, Louis Bertrand, and Don Bosco, to name but a few. They are concrete proof that the gift of healing has continued to be bestowed on individual members of the People of God throughout the ages.

Currently, also, in Protestant and Catholic Pentecostal groups there is a manifest presence of the gift of healing. And in talks with Catholic missionaries in Africa I have learned that there is a growing interest in the relationship between the proclamation of the Good News and healing. The African, it is reported, sees a natural connection between religion and healing. Fortunately, the tendency of various Christian churches to play down or ignore the vital relationship between authentic religion and healing is presently being overcome in Africa and elsewhere.

In the present context it is also important to stress that the Christian should be eager to acknowledge the presence of the healing Christ wherever it is manifested. In the past there was a tendency to deny that the gift of healing could be bestowed on individuals in Christian churches other than one's own. Yet, once it is acknowledged that there is an intrinsic connection between proclaiming the Good News and healing, then wherever and to the extent that Christ is authentically preached, his healing presence is likewise to be found. Moreover, Jesus himself urged his disciples to be very open in this matter. Mark, for example, reports that the apostles came to Christ complaining: "Master, we saw a man who is not one of us casting out devils in your name; and because he was not one of us we tried to stop him" (Mark 9:38). But Jesus replied: "You must not stop him: no one who works a miracle in my name is likely to speak evil of me. Anyone who is not against us is for us" (Mark 9:39-40). The authentic Christian presupposition, then, in regard to those who claim to heal or do good works in Christ's name should be one of humble openness and eagerness to recognize Christ's healing presence wherever it may be manifested.

The Sacraments

Sacrament for the Christian means a visible manifestation of the healing mercy and transforming grace of God. Jesus Christ himself is properly understood as *the* Sacrament because he is "the image of the unseen God" (Colossians 1:15) and the dynamic efficacious sign of the Father's saving love for men. In Jesus Christ, Paul writes, "lives the fulness of divinity" (Colossians 2:9), and through his saving work he has reconciled us to the Father.

After his death and resurrection, Jesus remained with his people through the sending of his Spirit and he now uses the Christian Church instrumentally as the extension of his incarnational presence in history, as the new sacramental sign of his saving presence. Just as through Christ the

Father's saving mercy and love was manifested to his people, so through the Church Jesus in his saving and enlightening power is present to mankind.

The Church is the fundamental sacrament and wellspring of what Christians ordinarily refer to as "the sacraments." This is so because the Church is the mystical body and bride of Christ and the visible, abiding, powerful, and effective sign-mystery of Christ's continuous loving presence in the world.

Individual sacraments, such as baptism, confirmation, the Eucharist and the others, are specific visible signs through which Christ is present and at work in his Church in varying manners. Each of the individual sacraments is unique in the peculiar fashion in which it makes the shape or form of Christ's invisible grace manifest.

The Christian churches vary in the number of specific sacraments which they acknowledge. Catholicism and the Eastern Church accept seven "peak-signs" of Christ's sacramental activity in his Church. Here I will look briefly at each of the seven sacraments in the context of healing through enlightenment. I realize, of course, that this is only one of any number of ways in which they can be viewed.

THE SACRAMENTS AS SIGNS THAT HEAL THROUGH ENLIGHTENMENT

Grounds for speaking of the sacraments as signs that "heal through enlightenment" are found both in the Hebrew and New Testaments, as well as in theological reflections approved by the Church.

For the Hebrews, Yahweh is often portrayed as bringing forth healing and newness of life through his light. When the Israelites fled from the bondage of the Egyptians, Yahweh went before them "by night in the form of a pillar of fire to give them light" (Exodus 13:21). The psalmist speaks of Yahweh as "my light and my salvation" (Psalm 27:1), and says, "with you is the fountain of life, / by your light we see the light" (Psalm 36:9). Isaiah comforts God's people by proclaiming that "Yahweh will be your everlasting light / and your days of mourning will be ended" (Isaiah 60:20), and the prophet Malachi speaks God's words to his people, saying "for you who fear my name, the sun of righteousness will shine out with healing in its rays; you will leap like calves going out to pasture" (Malachi 3:20).

In the event of Jesus Christ, according to Zechariah's Spirit-inspired words, Yahweh sends "the rising Sun to visit us, to give light to those who live in darkness and the shadow of death" (Luke 1:78-79). And for John the apostle, Jesus is the light that saves his people from darkness and transforms them into sons of light (John 12:36; 8:12). For Paul of Tarsus, the mystery of Jesus is to be seen as an unending source of salvation and enlightenment (Ephesians 1:18).

Since the sacraments are in fact the concrete manifestation in space and time of the constancy of the saving and healing work of Yahweh, and in these last days, of his Son, who gave life through his light, it follows that a certain healing and saving through light must be at the core of all sacramental activity.

A further ground for speaking of the sacraments as "healing through enlightenment" is found in the ultimately scripturally based and widely held theological view that the "sacraments cause by signifying." What this basically means is that the sacraments cause their proper effects by being signs and that they bring about exactly what they symbolize or signify. Thus, for example, baptism involves a washing, and this washing signifies and, as the instrument of Christ, actually produces an interior cleansing and transformation. The sacrament, accordingly, brings about its healing effect through its sign-value, or meaning. But since sign-value is literally meaningless apart from someone who understands the sign, it is in a profound sense the same thing to say that the sacraments "work by enlightening" as it is to say that they "cause by signifying." Of course, very subtle controversies regarding sacramental causality have raged for ages and cannot be done justice here. But the key point is nevertheless plain and true. Sacraments are *most* effective when they are administered and received by individuals who understand the meaning of the sacramental sign, respond to it in faith, and try to live it out in their lives. It remains to consider the individual sacraments as effective signs that bring healing and fullness of life through their light.

BAPTISM

Baptism is the sacrament of *radical* healing through enlightenment. Man is dead because of sin, but through the light of baptism he becomes alive in Christ. In New Testament writings baptism is referred to as receiving the light (Hebrews 6:4; 10:32). The Fathers of the Church also write of baptism as enlightenment. This view is expressed in the homilies of Cyril of Jerusalem, where those to be baptized are called "candidates for enlightenment." In the early Church, baptism required catechesis as a preparation for its reception, and after it was received still richer and deeper instructions in the meaning of the mysteries followed. These practices flowed from the insight that for the adult, enlightening faith in the healing Christ-meaning powerfully at work in the sacrament of baptism is required for its fruitful reception and leads to an ever richer experience of its grace once the sacrament is received.

In Scripture there is an intimate connection between faith and baptism. Paul ascribes the same effects to faith and baptism. In fact, baptism gives faith or inner enlightenment outward expression. Through faith in the healing power of Christ at work in baptism the one baptized wakes from his sleep, rises from the dead, and experiences the light of Christ shining on him (cf. Ephesians 5:14).

Baptism has the twofold effect of freeing from sin and death and filling with new life in Christ. Baptism accordingly is the sacrament of initiation into the Christian life. To all who live out the meaning of baptism, it becomes a constant source of strength and light, involving the constant renouncing of Satan and his works and continual openness in faith to the healing light of Christ first experienced in baptism. This is the joy and delight, the peace and well-being, the illumination and transformation, that come through baptism into the Lord.

CONFIRMATION

Baptism makes us participants in the death and resurrection of the Lord. Confirmation most basically communicates the grace of Pentecost. Both baptism and confirmation heal through enlightening. Through baptismal illumination the individual dies to sin and experiences a new birth and a basic consecration to the Lord. Through the grace and light of confirmation the human person is healed and strengthened in his ability to overcome his own weakness and to bear witness to Christ by transforming the world and bringing it into the Kingdom of God. Confirmation perfects the basic consecration of baptism and makes us mature members of the Body of Christ. The prayer of the bishop at confirmation reveals the Pentecostal dimension of the sacrament:

Almighty and eternal God, you have granted your servants to be born again from water and the Holy Spirit and have forgiven them all their sins. Send them your Holy Spirit from heaven, the Consoler, with his seven gifts. Amen. The Spirit of wisdom and understanding. Amen. The Spirit of counsel and fortitude. Amen. The Spirit of knowledge and piety. Amen. Fill them with the Spirit of your fear, and vouchsafe to seal them with the sign of Christ's cross unto eternal life.[4]

In confirmation growth in knowledge and wisdom and strength of heart is given. Baptism is thus not the end but the beginning of the enlightenment process. In confirmation the very Spirit of light and truth is given to one in yet a fuller and more manifest fashion. Through the enlightening power of confirmation, the Christian shares more fully in the wisdom and strength of Christ and in the light of this understanding goes forth to witness to the light that is life.

Like the graces of baptism, the graces of confirmation are constantly available to the baptized and confirmed Christians. Thus, just as the renewal of the baptismal vows brings a renewal of life to the Christian, calling upon the Pentecostal Spirit received in confirmation brings an increase in enlightenment and strength of heart. The Christian should often meditate upon the meaning of baptism and confirmation because, through this meditation, the healing and enlightening graces of the sacraments become ever more present to the meditator.

HOLY ORDERS

Through baptism individuals are incorporated into the People of God, which is a priestly people. Through confirmation Christians are strengthened through the Pentecostal Spirit in their union with Christ the priest, and receive the grace to bear mature witness to Christ and his saving deeds in the world. Through the fullness of the sacrament of Holy Orders, the bishop, and priests and deacons in varying degrees of participation, are consecrated to the service of the People of God as pastors, teachers of the word, and dispensers of the sacraments. The bishop acts in the name of Christ in the visibility of the Church and is thus called to be an instrument of healing through enlightening in his teaching, his governing, and his administration of various sacraments.

In the sacrament of holy orders, individuals are consecrated to a special way of life and receive the graces necessary to live out their special calling. Thus, the bishop, and priests and deacons as well, are called in an official fashion to be "other Christs," to announce Christ's healing word and to dispense the sacraments. Through holy orders they receive the healing and enlightening graces necessary to carry out that mission.

It is true that in the Catholic tradition, even serious sinfulness on the part of the minister of the sacrament does not prevent the sacraments from taking effect. It must be repeatedly emphasized, however, that the bishop and other ministers of the sacraments are most true to their calling and most effective in their ministry to the extent that they embody in themselves the healing through enlightenment which they preach and bring to others through the sacraments.

MARRIAGE

There is in the Church a sacrament of service and love in which two persons are consecrated for life to one another and to Christ. This is the sacrament of marriage. Whether marriage is considered a sacrament in the strict sense, or sacramental and symbolic in a looser sense, this union can be seen as a source of healing through enlightenment. Through it two persons who deeply love one another become "two in one flesh," and this mutual consecration is solemnized and sacralized in the Church.

The Christian community and most especially those committed to each other in Christian marriage are called constantly to reflect on the meaning of marriage and the rich significance of the sacramental consecration of two persons to each other and to Christ.

In Genesis marriage is portrayed in its ideal form as the monogamous union of "two in one flesh." The man and woman mutually fulfill one another and are joined together in a permanent union for the sake of loving companionship and the propagation of the race. Through sin, however, the Genesis ideal of marriage is weakened and a tragic element is introduced into marriage. In the Hebrew Testament the ideal of the perfect marriage is still praised but lesser practices are allowed and the ideals of Genesis are rarely attained.

In the sacrament of matrimony, however, Christ heals the ruptures in marital ideals brought about by original and personal sins, and provides the grace to individuals who maturely commit themselves to each other in Christian marriage to be faithful to each other until death. Yet more significantly, as Paul indicates in Ephesians, Christ makes his own love and fidelity to the Church the enlightening model for the love and commitment to which spouses are mutually called. Christ's "marriage" with his bride, the Church, thus becomes the exemplar and the enlightening source of grace for Christians who commit themselves in the marriage union. Moreover, just as Christ shows to spouses the way of authentic love and commitment, so the spouses are to provide for their children in their love and devotion to each other a model for authentic living and maturation.

Clearly, the sacrament of marriage, like the other sacraments, brings about healing and fulfillment through its sign-value. Christian married couples through the sacrament of matrimony are called and given the graces to manifest the very fidelity of Christ to his Church in their own married union. Christian marriage is a profound vocation,

and Christian married couples fulfill their matrimonial vocation in ever richer fashion to the extent that they grow in
an enlightened understanding of the mystery of Christ's
love for his Church and try to show this love in their own
union of love and in forming the image of Christ in their
children.

PENANCE, THE SACRAMENT OF RECONCILIATION

Although each of the sacraments involves a healing aspect, the sacrament of reconciliation, like baptism and the
anointing of the sick, has healing and restoration as its central function. There are multiple aspects under which the
healing work of this sacrament might be viewed. In the
present limited context of healing through enlightenment,
however, the focus is on the confession of one's sins
whether in the strict sacramental form of the Catholic tradition or in the other ways we admit and confess our sinfulness, as a particular sacral instance of what I term "the
healing law of self-manifestation."

The notion of the healing law of self-manifestation can be
seen in the writings of Sidney M. Jourard[5] and the approach of Alcoholics Anonymous. Jourard stresses that individuals tend to conceal rather than reveal themselves and
that this is the source of not a little sickness, misunderstanding, and alienation. In Alcoholics Anonymous, there is
likewise a great stress on self-disclosure. The famous
Twelve Steps of A.A. ask the individual, if he truly wishes
healing, to become transparent to himself and to his fellow
recovering alcoholics before God. The first steps in the
healing process for the alcoholic involve acknowledging his
powerlessness over alcohol to himself, to others, and to
God. Later steps require the making of a "fearless moral
inventory" and admitting to God, to oneself, and to another
human being the exact nature of one's wrongs. Clearly both

Jourard and A.A. acknowledge the radical healing power of self-manifestation. What takes place in the sacrament of reconciliation, through the confession of one's sins, is a particular instance of the general healing law of self-manifestation. It is, however, subsumed and integrated within an ecclesial and Christ-centered healing context.

The healing law of self-manifestation operative in the sacrament of reconciliation is a profound instance of healing through enlightenment. This is because self-manifestation is also self-revelation, or revelation of the self to the self, and this revelation heals. In other words, in the act of confessing, of manifesting oneself, a deeper understanding is born. Thus, for example, lovers come to a deeper understanding of their love by uttering it in words and attempting to articulate it. Likewise, the alcoholic in the moment of his acknowledgment of his alcoholism begins a process of ever deepening self-understanding. Enlightenment is accordingly found at the very heart of the healing law of self-manifestation.

Through self-manifestation there is an escape from the darkness of self-deception. There is no longer any need for the thousand flights from understanding through rationalization, repression, projection, compensation, and all the other devices of escape from the light of self-knowledge. Through self-manifestation then, and above all through the self-manifestation in the sacrament of reconciliation, an individual is freed from the schizophrenic condition of being one thing on the outside and another on the inside. When Jesus said that "there is nothing hidden but it must be disclosed, nothing kept secret except to be brought to light" (Mark 4:22), he was echoing the basic need and desire of man to let the outside be in harmony with the inside. Through confession, and the repentance and resolution to amend one's way of life which flow from it, the individual enters into an enlightened state of harmony with himself,

with others, and with God, and becomes a transparency
through which the pure light of God shines. Finally,
through the transforming power of the sacrament of reconciliation, the individual is healed not only of his spiritual
disharmony and interior opaqueness of heart, but also of
those psychic and bodily diseases which were the symp-
tomatic expressions of his spiritual disorder.

The sacrament of reconciliation involves both negating
and affirming aspects, but it is above all the positive elements which should be accentuated. True enough, penance
requires humility of heart, sorrow for sin and repentance,
but it is at its heart a joyous affair. Through sincere self-
manifestation in the sacrament of reconciliation the individual, like the prodigal son, "comes to his senses" and
returns to the Father. In the process of confession the individual is healed through a growth in self-knowledge and in
an ever deeper understanding of the unsearchable riches of
the Father's mercy and his light-filled forgiving love. The
conscience of the repentant sinner glows with the radiance
of intensified love and understanding as he realizes that he
was lost but is now found.

ANOINTING THE SICK

As Christ is present through the sacrament of reconciliation for healing the human spirit wounded by sin, he is
present just as he once was in Galilee, Jerusalem, and elsewhere as the healer of man's physical ills through the sacrament of the anointing of the sick. Thus, the sacrament of
the anointing of the sick was given to the Church as a sign
of Christ's desire to heal the whole person physically as well
as spiritually.

Perhaps the best place to begin a discussion of the sacrament of anointing is with the classic text of James:

If one of you is ill, he should send for the elders of the church, and they must anoint him with oil in the name of the Lord and pray over him. The prayer of faith will save the sick man and the Lord will raise him up again; and if he has committed any sins, he will be forgiven.

James 5:14-15

Exegesis of this passage has varied in the past, but contemporary interpretations tend more to agree that the primary intent of the rite of anointing spoken of by James is that of the healing of bodily sickness. It is significant to note that here the anointing may also effect the forgiveness of sin, even serious sin, but this is not its primary purpose, since from the text of James it is clear that the individual who receives the anointing is not automatically presumed to be guilty of this or that particular sin.

In the sacrament of the anointing there is a healing through enlightenment just as there is in the other sacraments. The particular enlightening grace of the sacrament of the anointing would appear to be an interior illumination, a deepening of trust and a strengthening in spirit which permeates effectively the psychic, emotional, and physical dimensions of the person and either restores the individual to health or enables the individual to so transcend his illness that he is freed from emotional or mental bondage to it.

It is important to realize that the type of illness James refers to in the passage cited above is not the illness of the moribund but of the seriously ill. In the early Church this crucial point was clearly understood and has always been so understood by the Eastern Orthodox churches, with the exception of the Nestorians, who do not accept the anointing of the sick as a sacrament. From about the twelfth century, however, up to very recent times, the sacrament of the anointing in the Roman Catholic Church came to be viewed primarily both on the theological and pastoral level as the sacrament of "extreme unction." The appearance of the priest at the sick bed came to be viewed as the sign of the imminence of death rather than of likely healing. If Leslie Weatherhead is correct, it came to the point in some instances where the person who received extreme unction was expected to die, and if he did not die, then in certain matters he had to live as if he were already dead. He could not marry and he was not permitted to change his will.[6] It is, of course, true that it is not God's will that every individual who receives the sacrament of the anointing should recover from his illness. For some the sacrament provides those graces which enable the individual to accept death and to die in Christ full of hope and love. The primary aim of the sacrament, however, as it is described in James' epistle, is to bring about the healing of the individual from his illness.

Happily, at Vatican II the expression "anointing of the sick" was once again employed to describe the sacrament and various pastoral reforms were set in motion. Much, however, remains to be done in terms of the development of an adequate theology of the sacrament of the anointing and the implementation of reforms on the pastoral level. Unfortunately, many Catholics today still lack a true understanding of the meaning and significance of the sacrament of anointing. As a result, they do not ask for it when they are seriously ill, nor do they have an authentic understanding of its sign-value when they receive it. This means, of course, since the sacraments cause by signifying, that if the individual thinks that he is being visited by the angel of death instead of the healing Christ, he is quite likely to throw up a tremendous psychic block against the effective functioning of the sacrament as a sign. One hopes, however, that a proper catechesis regarding the true nature of the sacrament will be carried out on a large scale, and

Christians will come to recognize in an ever richer fashion the dynamic presence of the healing Christ in the sacrament of the anointing.

THE HOLY EUCHARIST

The sacraments of initiation and consecration raise Christians to new and fuller levels of existence and service. The sacraments of forgiveness and recovery heal the wounds of sin so that those who receive the sacraments may serve the Lord with renewed dedication and health. These sacraments, together with those of holy orders and matrimony and all the varied gifts of the Spirit, manifest the light, peace, joy, and salvation of the Lord at work in the People of God throughout the world.

The Holy Eucharist is the sacrament of healing through enlightenment par excellence because it is the very presence under the sacramental sign of Christ himself—the healing light—and of his saving sacrifice. It is from the Eucharist that all the other sacraments flow as from their fount and source. And because the Eucharist is the center of the life of the Church, Christians should seek constantly through prayer and meditation to grow in a loving understanding of the inexhaustible riches of the Eucharist.

The Holy Eucharist is the richest in meaning of all the sacraments because in it meaning itself, the Logos made flesh, is present to us under the sacramental sign. The Eucharist, like the diamond, is multifaceted, but three of the most important ways in which it may be viewed are as love feast, sacrifice, and thanksgiving.

The Eucharist is a love feast which joins together in an ever deepening bond of love all the members of the People of God who are alive in Christ. Together in the liturgy of the word the members of the People of God listen to the wisdom of the revealed word and through a living faith "eat" this word, are nourished by it and strengthened in their love of God and their love for one another. In the liturgy of the bread the community of the faithful joyously partake in the new Passover Meal—the messianic banquet —and by sharing in the sacrifice of Christ and eating his flesh and drinking his blood are ever more profoundly transformed into Christ and joined to one another in love.

The Eucharist is a *sacrificial* love feast. In the Eucharist, Christ's sacrifice on Calvary is made present to us in a true way and through the mystery of the Eucharist event the Church recalls, participates in, and proclaims the death and resurrection of the Lord. For the Christian then to celebrate the Eucharistic banquet is to share in the fruits of Christ's sacrifice and all its healing effects. Through the Eucharist, Christ heals his people of their wounds, nourishes them with his own life, transforms them into himself and makes them grow in an ever deeper union with one another as members of his Body.

The Eucharist is a thanksgiving. Through the Eucharistic sacrificial banquet the Christian is made to share in the very thanksgiving and praise which Jesus offers forever to the Father. At a key moment in the Eucharist, the Christian prays: "Through him and with him and in him is to you, God the Father Almighty, in the unity of the Holy Spirit, all honor and glory forever. Amen." In the Eucharist the Christian's prayer of adoration and thanksgiving becomes a foretaste of that moment when God's Kingdom shall be fully revealed and all the redeemed and the glorified shall join in an ecstatic hymn of praise to the Father and to the Lamb. The Eucharist, then, is a pledge of future glory and an anticipative participation even now in the everlasting marriage feast of the Lamb.

Finally, though the Eucharist is a memorial of the past and a pledge of the glory that is to come, it is a healing and enlightening happening in the present for the People of

God. Thus, each day in the liturgy of the word the Good News of Christ's healing work is effectively announced to the Christian, and in the liturgy of the bread Christ's healing sacrifice is powerfully at work for his people. Because the healing Christ is so wonderfully and effectively present in the Eucharistic sacrifice and banquet, the prayers of the liturgy abound in petitions for deliverance from all evils and for every type of healing and fullness of life. Thus, for example, right after the recitation of the Lord's Prayer, the priest prays: "Deliver us, Lord, from every evil . . . and protect us from all anxiety." And again, before partaking in the sacrificial meal, the priest and people pray: "Lord, I am not worthy to receive you, but only say the word and I shall be healed." And the priest prays that by receiving the Lord with faith in His love and mercy he may receive "health in mind and body." The Eucharist, then, is *the* sacrament of healing through enlightenment because, when it is received and shared in with the living light of faith, it frees individuals from all evils and fills the spiritually hungry with an abundance of good things.

NOTES

A.

1. I italicize this phrase to emphasize that although in a sin-free world man might still have "died" in some sense, nonetheless sickness, suffering, and death *as* they are presently given in human experience are due to man's sin.

B.

1. Irenaeus, *Adversus haereses*, II, ch. xxii.

2. Origen, *Contra Celsum*, III, ch. xxiv.

3. Augustine, *City of God: The Fathers of the Church* (New York: Fathers of the Church, Inc., 1954), XXIV, pp. 447–450.

4. *A New Catechism* (New York: Herder and Herder, 1969), p. 256.

5. Sidney M. Jourard, *Disclosing Man to Himself* (New York: Van Nostrand Reinhold Company, 1968).

6. Leslie D. Weatherhead, *Psychology, Religion and Healing* (Nashville: Abingdon Press, 1951), p. 85.